DIARY OF A
DIVORCED MOTHER

DIARY OF
A DIVORCED
MOTHER

Marilyn Murray Willison

WYDEN BOOKS

For my parents

301.92
Dm
4/80

MANUFACTURED IN THE UNITED STATES OF AMERICA

FIRST EDITION

Library of Congress Cataloging in Publication Data

Willison, Marilyn Murray.
      Diary of a divorced mother.

      1. Willison, Marilyn Murray. 2. Divorcées—
United States—Biography. 3. Single parents—United
States—Biography. I. Title.
HQ834.W6253   301.42′84′0924 [B]   79-66071
ISBN 0-87223-577-7

"Every writer knows that somehow, somewhere you talk your stories first, or they talk *you*. You begin to feel something you have to say something about and you *hear* yourself and it stops you like a red light or a bugle blowing. A writer is never more than twenty-six letters away from putting it *down* on paper. Nor is he ever allowed scruples . . . . The worst of burying things you don't like to think about for years is that when they do come up it is as though the subconscious had kept them as fresh as a freezer. So I am glad to get this out in the open, to see it more plainly now . . . though I will try very hard to be fair . . . it is only right to admit that I saw through the eyes of young indignant hostility and horror."

—Adela Rogers St. Johns,
Final Verdict

Contents

Contents

DIARY OF A
DIVORCED MOTHER

1

Too Stubborn to Say Good-bye to Suburbia

The newspapers and magazines go out of their way to remind us that the nuclear family is creeping toward extinction. They say that 40 percent (or more) of today's children will grow up spending at least a portion of their youth in a single-parent home. For adults like me, who grew up in real-life Walt Disney neighborhoods—where daddies went to work, mommies went to PTA, and kids went to school and Scouts—it's an unsettling prediction.

Although I am surrounded by announcements that America is now the land of the singles, I don't see it that way. I see that in my little corner of suburbia I am a "novelty" in the neighborhood because I live in a husbandless house. I ignored my friends' well-meaning advice after my divorce—they strongly urged me to sell the house and move to a different place designed for (and hospitable to) singles. My friends felt that staying in the same neighborhood that had spawned my husband's departure, seeing the old crowd that was now too uncomfortable to include me in its marrieds-only socializing, and being a divorced working mother in the midst of stay-at-home mommies would prove difficult. They were right.

But, as with most difficult situations, there are a few silver linings; they are small glimpses that let me believe that I just may turn into a survivor, after all. The feeling I have is not a "for sure" or "definitely." It's just a "maybe"—but it's enough to make the difference between giving up and not giving up.

In the neighborhood where I live, my children are the only ones who return home from school, day after day, to a baby-sitter. During my growing-up years I never experienced coming home to anyone—ever—except my mother. And she was almost always in the kitchen wearing an apron, waiting to hear about the ups and downs of my day. Just when I was developing a strong case of the terminal guilts because afternoons (and mornings) found me working in an office, my son told me he liked the fact that I had a career. It gave him, he said, a more unusual type of mom; besides, he'd learned a lot of Spanish from the baby-sitter. It made him, he said, unique—because no one else in his whole class lived the way we did and he thought that was "neat." His casual remark saved me a great deal of useless guilt. It also reminded me to save my strength for worries about real problems—not make-believe ones.

At kindergarten open house last fall I learned that my five-year-old son was the only child who did not have a daddy at home. As I strolled among the miniature desks gazing at the rather primitive family portraits each child had drawn, I was terrified that my son might have suffered trauma or embarrassment because he—and his home—was different. I released an audible sigh of relief when I saw his picture: It consisted of smiling, colorful stick drawings of "mommy, big brother, and me." It was almost as if he—

unlike his mother—was unconcerned about the fact that our little family is daddyless.

On my older son's hockey team, every boy has both a mother and a father at home—every boy except my son. The normal arrangement is for the mothers to make coffee and sponsor bake sales and for the fathers to play goal judge or timekeeper. There are two adults in each family to handle the predawn schlepping back and forth between home and ice rink. The bad news is that since my husband moved out I've had twice as much driving and twice as many hockey jobs; the good news is that there have been twice as many "Thanks mom—you were great" smiles from my son. I've had the serendipitous benefit of learning how to be a goal judge, lace ice skates, spot fouls, and catch a check with the best of them. And I've had the good luck to be pushed into a part of my son's life I would always have missed if I had a husband.

I won't deny that since the departure of the "man-around-the-house" we have had more work, less money, less pampering, and less predictability in our day-to-day life. But those everyday hassles have forced our family to grow closer with a touching and endearing intimacy we never had before. There is a great deal more humor and growth and respect in this house because we've each learned what we really need for survival: love and each other.

Okay, my sons don't have an everyday father, I don't have a supportive husband, and our family has a lot of bills and not much money in the bank. But when the suburbanites wonder how long we'll hold out before selling the house and giving up the struggle, I mentally thumb my nose at their skepticism. Let them feel sorry for—or scornful of—us because there's no man in our lives. It's going to take much more than the departure of a man to undermine the stubbornness and love that we have at our house. My boys and I, you see, have a secret—we know that as long as we have each other, nothing can get us down.

And so far, nothing has.

2

---◦◦◦◦---

Advice I Wish Somebody Had Given Me

I've always been skeptical of social theories and advanced opinions claiming to predict human behavior. The iconoclast in me rebels at the thought that the human species is no more special than lemmings or honeybees.

But I'll admit that when it comes to divorce I have been wrong. What little I was told about being a single mother wasn't too far off the mark. What I was told was good—it just wasn't enough; now I'd like to share some advice I *wish* I'd received.

I wish someone had told me not to expect my social life to stay the way it was when I was married. For some reason, it seems, whether in a big city or a burg, married people tend to associate with married people, single people with singles, and only the oldest, dearest friends dare to break this convention. I wish I'd been warned that invitations to married friends' homes would go something like this: "Fred will be out of town on Friday, so why don't you come over?" I wish I'd known that I'd wind up meeting my married girl friends only for lunch or at large parties until, eventually, I hardly ever saw them at all.

It would also have been nice to know that I would develop an entirely new set of friends—single, divorced, widowed, who were not uncomfortable because I was husbandless. These people know how to cope with the difficult aspects of single life and how to enjoy the good ones. If, during the transition stage of losing the "old" crowd of married friends, I'd known I would make a whole new set of rewarding friendships, I might not have felt so forlorn.

I also wish I'd been told not to worry about my children taking sides. The fact that my ex-husband had a lot more money than I left me in a state of panic. I worried that his expensive toys or late-model cars might lure my children away from me. I wish I'd known that children form their own versions of who did what (and why) regardless of input from adults. In fact, my older son knew that there had been smoke in the pantry long before I did. I wish I'd known enough to trust in my sons' ability to love me—and my ex—from a biological as well as intellectual framework.

Not too many children these days complete their education without being touched—directly or indirectly—by divorce. I should have known that my little ones would learn how to strike a comfortable balance between their estranged parents. I wish I'd always been able to remember that their love was too deep to be "bought"—then I could have relaxed instead of wasting my time with groundless worries. It would have helped to have known that giving children the freedom to feel comfortable at the beginning of a divorce helps them to help adults with adult feelings later—when we need strength the most. I wish someone had reminded me that children are a lot smarter (when it comes to divorce) than adults think.

I wish someone had told me not to expect my ex's family

to remain as cordial as it had been before the divorce. I should have known that if you wanted the breakup, you've hurt your spouse's parents' feelings by hurting their child. If their child wanted the breakup, parents can't help but wonder what you did to make their baby behave that way. I wish I'd been advised that it would be best to maintain a distant, civilized relationship and to stop holding my breath waiting for offers of help or "Honey, we love you's." I wish I'd been told that the only thing we would have in common to talk about would be the grandchildren, and that the deadweight of a new daughter-in-law would hang heavy in the air between us.

I wish I'd known that it would be folly to expect my employer to be understanding about my plight as a single mother. Bosses have, I have since learned, the tendency to think that a single parent has the freedom of a single person while retaining the dependability of a married employee. Wrong—with a capital W—on both counts. No one told me that I'd be filling the shoes of a mommy and a daddy every day of my life—whether I went to the office or not. I wish I'd been told that my employer was not really prepared to understand (or be interested in) why I might have to rush off to daytime parent-teacher conferences; why I would have to chauffeur my sons to the doctor or the dentist; or why I would have to make certain phone calls during business hours. No one told me that unless I was very, very careful I would appear less "professional" than my co-workers (or bosses), who either had spouses to share child-care duties or were childless.

The most valuable tip I could have received is the message that no one could deliver. The biggest boost, you see, would have been in knowing that I would not remain—in any way—the person I was when we were a traditional nuclear family. No one told me that my divorce would be an education—about life, emotions, money, most of all about me. After my one-year "Oh my God, what happened?" period of shock and depression, I had no idea that I might emerge a more confident, happier person. No one told me that there is a great deal to be said about the challenge of meeting life head on—and surviving to talk about it.

I wish I'd been told that I would—eventually—feel proud of my newfound sense of independence merely because it would be something I'd been forced to earn the hard way. And even in these divorce-prone days, the old adage still applies: What we earn invariably possesses greater value than what we're given.

3

Friday Nights and Single Mothers

It's 10 P.M. Friday. My sons and I have watched "The Incredible Hulk" and "Wonder Woman" surrounded by their Ovaltine, my needlepoint, and our popcorn. I've shooed them upstairs, supervised the change into pajamas, and have inspected the fluoride-brushed teeth and the freshly washed faces. A (short) bedtime story has been told, and good-night kisses have been traded all around.

Finally the house is quiet, the week is over, and, like most Friday nights of late, I am alone with coffee and my end-of-the-week thoughts. There was a time, I remember, when Friday nights meant fun—a reward for having survived the weekday rigors of school and/or work. A Friday night alone—back then—would have been a blatant admission of failure to produce friends—male or female—who wanted the pleasure of my company. Now, I ruefully admit that I can't imagine wanting anything more from a Friday night than solitude and sleep. I think single mothers are too tired on Friday nights to read about—much less practice—the fascination of womanhood.

Quiet Friday nights are almost always my most productive personal time. After a week at the office, nights crammed with homework and hockey and housecleaning, I have a few quiet hours alone—just for me—before I am inundated with the ebullient presence of my friends and my sons' friends. It's as if Friday nights have become a breather between the onslaught of two different storms— and I wouldn't have it any other way.

This Friday night, however, is different. My lunch hour today was spent with four girl friends—two divorced and two never married. These women were discussing which "watering holes" to visit tonight and which places were most likely to provide "a meaningful encounter." Euphemisms aside, they were comparing notes on L.A.'s many singles bars. The women, knowing all too well my inbred aversion to smoky bars, inebriated attempts at conversation, and Friday nights away from home, perfunctorily invited me to join them tonight. I, equally perfunctorily, declined. This pattern has been repeated countless times since my husband moved out, just as the Monday lunch hour rehash of who-met-whom-where Friday night.

But today was different. Today, over salad, one of the women said, "You probably think you're going to get some kind of motherhood medal for staying home tonight with two little kids and stooping to their level of conversation." I mused that it might be a nice idea. "Well," she continued, "you'll never get one that way. Those boys don't need you and your bedtime stories. They need a man in the house. Wrapping yourself around them and their childish needs isn't going to get them a new daddy. You're not helping them and you're not helping yourself by sitting in the suburbs sipping Ovaltine. Friday night you belong out of the house, with people your own age, meeting men and learning how to judge and be judged in the singles market. You don't need TV and popcorn and preschoolers. You need a husband."

Feeling chastened and confused, I told her I'd think about it, that maybe this time I would meet them later at Monahan's or Casey's or Bergen's. Or maybe I wouldn't.

I returned to my desk after lunch feeling like a relic from the Pleistocene age masquerading as a twenty-nine-year-old in Los Angeles. My instincts were hopelessly out of step with the Mr. Goodbar life-style that's been carved out for singles.

My friend's well-meaning, if harsh, accusation that I wasn't helping myself or my sons still rings in my ears. It's hard for me to think that my children really need me to advertise for a new husband more than they need my attention and my time. I don't happen to think they do—but how can I be sure?

The Monday morning rehash will probably sound the same to the regular foursome who were "there" on Friday night. For me, this week, it may sound altogether different.

I wish there were someone I could ask, "What's right for a mother?"

4

---·◁∞▷·---

The "Real" Me

I have a friend who did not discover that he had been adopted until he was twenty years old. When he went to enlist in the British army, a mixup of birth certificates resulted in a clerk announcing, "You surely were adopted, or else your birth records would be right here." Returning home from London stunned, he told his mother what had happened. She admitted—for the very first time—that he had come to live with them when he was a baby. Can you imagine his shock?

Unlike my friend, I sensed from my earliest memories that I was adopted. Perhaps the absence of baby photos, the zillions of photos of me as a preschooler (as if there had been no me, and then there could not be enough of me), and the goofs of chronology my parents would occasionally make gave me the feeling that I had surely not been with them from birth. Although my childish inquiries were either ignored or deflected, it was obvious that in spite of my parents' desire to wish away reality, I simply was not their "real" daughter.

Later, under the stars on the veranda of a Memphis

hotel while I was on vacation, a cousin asked me how I felt about being adopted and whether or not it bothered me. Although I was taken aback by her frankness—no one had ever asked me that question before—I was at the same time relieved to have verbal confirmation of what I'd always known deep down inside.

When I returned home to California I told my parents what had been said; they were surprised and despondent. It never occurred to them that relatives might not be discreet and they had hoped I would never "know" that my suspicions were correct. From the looks on their faces and the tone of voice in which they acknowledged my statements, I knew that my revelation had hurt them to the core. Shamefacedly, and with a great deal of regret for being so insensitive, I resolved never to mention it again.

After my father's death, my mother told me that the adoption had been his idea and that as far as he was concerned they were my "real" parents. Period. The thought that someone would later claim me or that I might conduct a frenzied search for my so-called "real" parents unsettled and unnerved him; he believed that the people who raised you—and loved you day in and day out—*were* your "real" parents. And in time I found myself in total agreement.

And yet. Although my parents loved me lavishly, I spent most of my teen years longing for an "identity." As the anomalous only "only child" among my Catholic girls school's families of five, six, or seven offspring, I longed to have someone in my family who looked like me. Sitting at my friends' dinner tables I would glance from face to face and make mental checklists of who had the mother's features, who had the dad's, and which kids merely looked like an amalgam of their siblings. And when I returned home it remained all too obvious that while I might have my father's personality or my mother's stubborn streak, physically I was cut from decidedly different fabric. My swarthy black Irish father and my petite red-haired mother bore little likeness to the tall, olive-skinned girl they had chosen to be their daughter.

The desire to find my "real" parents—an all-consuming preoccupation in my teens—diminished as I grew older. When still a girl, I spent long hours imagining how beautiful my mother was and how dashing and heroic my father must have been. I convinced myself that someone had, perhaps, taken me from them and they had spent the years grieving for their stolen daughter. I attached great significance to tall, brunette women who "looked like" they could be related to me. I hoped that someday, somehow, a woman would show up and straightforwardly say, "You don't know me, Marilyn, but I'm your mother." I knew in my heart of hearts that we would throw ourselves into each other's arms and love each other dearly. I also knew that a far more realistic version probably existed, one in which I had been a source of embarrassment or inconvenience to someone and that I was a distant, painful memory best left forgotten.

By the time I married, I was still curious about my "real" parents, but I was no longer obsessed. And by the time I'd had my first son, I wondered far more about the name and nationality than the personalities involved. By then I'd come to terms with my mother's story about how I'd come to live with them.

My father had been visiting Oregon on a business trip. He stayed at a hotel and the woman who owned the hotel introduced him to me. I was three. Neighbors of the landlady had asked her to baby-sit me for "a few hours." I was just under a year old. She agreed and was then shocked to find that they never came back and had, incredibly, moved with no forwarding address. She kept me with her, hoping they would return. By the time my father came on the scene she had decided that she would soon have to place me in an orphanage—it was obvious that my "real" parents were not going to reappear.

My father, as the story goes, fell in love with me and wired my mother that he had found "the perfect daughter." He urged her to catch the next train for Portland; she did, and soon I was living with them. After my fourth birthday the "probation" period was over and I was legally theirs.

Among the dim memories of my childhood is a picture of going with my mother to a man's office (it must have been the attorney who handled the adoption) and hearing him tell my mother how polite I was and remembering my mother's delight at his compliment.

My favorite hazy recollection of that period is of a gigantic shopping spree that resulted in hat boxes, lots of new shoes, unlimited new dresses, and a pale blue coat with a fur muff and matching hood. There is no doubt in my mind that the shopping spree that took place when I was about four years old is directly responsible for my lifelong passion for clothes.

Soon after my father's funeral Mama displayed a need to exorcise her feelings about what had hitherto been a secret. She developed a habit of dividing her reminiscences into "Before we adopted you" and "After we adopted you"— as if an excess of honesty would compensate for years of elusiveness. The change was so unexpected and so jarring that at one point I found myself hugging my mother in the middle of Saks and asking her please not to "remind" me anymore. We both had tears in our eyes and we both agreed—enough already.

By the time I married, I was still curious about my "real" parents, but I wasn't driven. Yet all through my first pregnancy, when I dealt with an Rh factor problem, incomplete medical histories, and other complications, I longed to tell the doctors brusquely that they should stop asking questions because the only answer I would ever be able to give them was "I don't know." After politely reminding them again and again that I was adopted, I resorted to shrugs and left it at that.

When we brought our baby home from the hospital, wearing his funny little yellow outfit that I'd knitted, I blissfully realized that for the very first time in my life I had a real honest-to-God family. Finally, at last, there was a someone in the world who was tied to me by blood. Like most things that people born into "normal" families take for granted, this was thrilling for me.

Nowadays, ordinary offhand comments about my sons— and the resemblance we are rumored to share—elicit an unusual response from me. When people say "he has your nose" or "I know where he got those dimples," I feel an inner glow that is beyond words. People who say those things cannot know that my mind translates it as a validation that I belong, that I am connected, that even though I am divorced, my "real" parents remain anonymous, and my adopted parents are dead, I still have family. A real family!

Perhaps the strongest legacy of my one-time fear of "familylessness" is my habit of promoting friends to family status. Instead of one or two sisters, I have many. My "pretend" family circle gets larger and larger each year, and I console myself that my family, such as it is, is composed of people I've chosen, something few people can say about their relatives.

When my husband moved out, I mourned more than just the loss of a mate. I mourned the loss of "belonging" and I knew that, once again, I would probably waste a great deal of time wondering what was "wrong" with me. I envied the security that went with his large family and her large family, while I was left to face a custody battle over the only two family members I had. Just as when I'd been a schoolgirl, I felt outnumbered and different and saddened by the fact that I had no home to return to and no one to call "mine." Once again, someone who was "supposed" to love me had decided not to.

Now that the battle is over, and my sons and I no longer have to worry about being taken from each other, I have, I think, come to grips with my adoption. These days it is enough to simply be grateful that I once had two loving parents and now am blessed with two sons to love.

As long as I'm making confessions, yes, I still wonder about my "real" parents. Although I would never have openly searched for them while my adoptive parents were alive, their death has removed the possibility of disappointing them. Nothing stops me from going to Portland, birth certificate in hand, and trying to solve the biggest mystery of my life. But still I don't go. I carry the Adoptees' Liberty Movement Association phone number in my wallet so that I always have the hot line to call for advice should I try to initiate contact with my "real" parents. But still I don't call.

There is, after all these years, a fear inside me that says it would be worse to know that the people who left me with a sitter might still not want me than it is never to know for sure. I wonder how I would feel if I were the natural mother involved—and I think about what she might feel about the daughter she once had. I fantasize about spotting her walking on the street—someone who looks like me—and I try to convince myself that seeing her would be enough. That seeing her would take away the need to introduce myself or ask questions or seek explanations. But I know myself well enough to know that a look or a glimpse would *not* be enough. And I know other people well enough to know that the reemergence of a phantom daughter could throw too many monkey wrenches into lives that are, at best, beset by troubles of their own. So I do the next best thing; I channel those thoughts and that energy into my own little family and I try to forget about the family that once was mine.

It is still annoying when others chide me for spending too much time or energy or effort on my boys. And it's unsettling to hear other mothers lament that "a son is only a son until he takes a wife." And I still ache when the boys have to divvy up their holiday time between their father and me. But I continue to console myself with the knowledge that even though I must share my children, occasionally relinquish them, and eventually teach them to be men with their own separate lives, they will always remain an integral part of the "real" me. The only part I will probably ever be able to know.

5

I'm Thirty Years Old.
Thirty? Thirty!

A look at the calendar (and the mirror) confirms that today is my thirtieth birthday. Although quite a few of my friends proudly claim that they crossed "the threshold" without the batting of an eye, I have a hodgepodge of conflicting thoughts on arriving at the big 3-o. While I'll reluctantly admit that I secretly scrutinize my face and figure and hair for signs of incipient old age, the biggest changes seem to be the ones that neither Laszlo, nor jogging, nor Vidal Sassoon affects. I am most intrigued by what makes me different now, at thirty, from the me of one or two decades ago.

If I were still married, the changes would be far fewer. But I am not, I am thirty, I am alone, and I have two small youngsters dependent on me for most of the things money can buy, and practically all of the things it can't.

I was raised by my dear, deceased parents to be a certain type of woman. Of necessity I now find I've evolved into an entirely different breed. My mother would probably be aghast; my father would probably be proud. Anne Morrow Lindbergh is the closest role model I can drum up for what my parents hoped for me (and I, always one to cooperate, hoped for myself). That "me" was raised to be literate, fluent, possess a certain savoir-faire and sensitivity, and, above all, make a good marriage. Writing (or other work) was fine as a sideline—as long as it remained a sideline. The ethereal, subliminally romantic prose of letters and diaries grew out of my life then, and, as if to demonstrate that it is easier to hang on to outworn habits than change them, even now I continue to keep a journal. It is the only part of my writing that reminds me of an earlier, easier life.

During my twenties, my husband (and his investments/ travels/career) ran like a wide swath through the fabric of my thoughts and my writing. My life with him in those days was, like my writing at that time, dignified and stately and lovely to behold. I wasn't even aware that I was clinging to him, and the security he represented, for dear life.

But that was then, and this is now. Now I find myself looking back at that era as a pretty part of my past that would no more sustain me today than a straight diet of Baskin-Robbins, Rocky Road flavor. The me of today is far less occupied with frills and much more aware of mounting responsibilities (both to myself and to others) than ever. I'm actually ashamed of the energy I squandered in a futile attempt to cling to a life I'd long ago outgrown.

These days, whenever I have spare time to think about the direction of my life, I find myself identifying with a crustier version of a female writer—someone less like Anne Morrow Lindbergh and more like Adela Rogers St. Johns (sorry, mom). I identify far more with a woman who needs to work than with one who has never had to wrestle with worries about paying the bills. Although I still happily retreat to *A Gift from the Sea* whenever I feel the need for a nonchemical tranquilizer, it seems that there is precious little time for philosophizing these days. A paycheck is essential—not only to my self-esteem but, more importantly, to my sustenance and my children's. A published article no longer means a decision about which antique, or dress, or dish to buy. But then I'm a much different woman at thirty than I was at twenty. My days as a UCLA co-ed feel as if they happened light-years ago, my perspective about practically everything (from welfare to motherhood to romance) has altered so drastically. I have aged in spite of my determination to remain fresh, to remain young, to remain unbiased. Perhaps I am learning that "remaining" is the nemesis of passing time—time does march on and, like it or not, insists on taking you (and your values) with it.

Motherhood has surely been responsible for a lot of growth, but divorce has been the primary architect of the decade's changes. Some will call me foolhardy, but I swear that divorce has passed over me like an enlightening illness—inflicting painful memories and scars; but leaving me grateful still to be among the living, confident that nothing—*nothing*—will ever prove as devastating. It has altered the way I perceive both the past and the future, which is what every difficult educating process should do.

I find I have a much higher fear threshold because I'm forced to appear brave; there are no alternatives. The side benefit of such mock bravado is that the goblins I had worried about as a greenhorn divorcée are much more pleasant in reality than they were in my imagination. They're not to be taken lightly, but I'm not nearly as frightened by them now as I was a few short years ago.

I no longer see life through rose-colored glasses, but I sense that I see things much more clearly now. I have learned, albeit against my will, that life is not a series of games—it is serious business. Lives and loves and children are at stake. I value so many things now—getting the bills paid, bubble baths, goofy times with my boys—that I once took for granted. I didn't know how fragile things were when I was a decade younger, and I'm afraid I didn't cherish or protect them as I would now.

So. Here I am a thirty-year-old. I've been forced—often against my will—to get to know myself and my capabilities as never before. Perhaps that's what the bugaboo about turning thirty is all about in the first place. It has a lot less to do with wrinkles and stray gray hairs than it has to do with filling in cracks and holes in the never-ending journey toward adulthood. I think a lot more concrete will be needed to complete this job—but today, divorced and thirty, I feel well on my way.

6

At Home with Tradition at Karen's House

I'm a hopeless traditionalist. Each birthday in our home calls for a gala celebration. The holidays, big and small, are feted—sometimes in a mindless way that causes me to repeat what I've done before (not necessarily because it is good or worthy, but because I've done it year after year with no negative repercussions). Surviving a divorce has, among other things, propelled me into a more analytical frame of mind. I'll admit I may not drastically change my actions all that much—but I do stop to think about my knee-jerk traditionalism. Before, I never did.

One of my favorite traditions has always been baking for the holidays. I used to bake at first as the person who helped my mother; in later years, I became the person my mother helped. As a child I felt confident that if I baked beside her and watched long enough I'd learn how to make delicate cakes, flawlessly textured breads, and perfect pies. I never did equal her high standards but I learned a lot during those marathon baking days—a lot about food and a lot about women. Ever since mama's death a few years ago—so unexpected at the age of sixty-nine—I find myself remembering and thinking about her almost every day. I particularly miss her before (more than during) the holidays; I miss our traditional all-day baking sessions in the kitchen and I miss the mother/daughter conversations that went along with them.

To help assuage that loneliness, the year after my mother's death, I sought the sanctuary of my high school classmate Karen to bake and listen and remind me that even though my family had dwindled to the point where the members could be counted on one hand, I was not alone. Together, each holiday season Karen and I chop and mix and stir and bake; we also do a lot of confiding and gossiping and giggling. We've cheerfully continued the tradition of baking together before the holidays, and now we look to each other to share the feelings and activities for that time of year that women of other generations shared with their mothers.

Since my family is so small, Karen is the closest link to my pubescent years—years we spent together at a girls' school with uniforms, demerits, and never-ending questions about boys, romance, boys, sophistication, boys, the real world, boys, and thoughts of how different we would someday be from our mildly unsatisfactory mothers. Our friendship managed to survive the journey from preteenagers all the way into adulthood—we each married, had children, and are now, so they tell us, women instead of girls.

The big difference between us is that I am divorced. I work away from the home each day, and I am raising my two boys to the best of my ability, alone. Karen is still happily married to her husband of twelve years. She works every day, but her title is housewife, and she and her husband center their energies on their two sons and a daughter. Each time I drive to Ventura to visit Karen and her family I feel I'll be a better person when I leave. Their small-town placidity is separated by light-years from my harried, never-quite-caught-up life in the city. Her children rarely watch TV—certainly never on school nights (they didn't even know who Mork and Mindy are). The family never misses church; both Karen and her husband serve as Sunday school teachers. Life at their house centers around not what's best for any one individual, but what's best for the entire family: soccer practice, piano lessons, and quiet evenings shared with five people who love each other.

Meals are nutritious, homemade, and innovative—no cake mix, instant pudding, or TV dinner has seen the inside of Karen's kitchen. If she can't make it cheaper, healthier, and better by doing it herself, it just doesn't get made. Needless to say, the house is efficient, orderly, and, quite unlike my home, blissfully quiet. Everything has its place, and everyone has his or her chore. It's so traditional middle-class America that I frequently feel that their way of life will soon follow the lead of mastodons, and Ethiopian egrets.

Karen manages cheerfully to care for her family without Spanish-speaking help. Without est. Without a shrink. She more than manages—she flourishes. And her husband enjoys the secure knowledge that he has the best homemaker in Ventura County to come home to each night. I swear each word of what I've written is true, but as I read this I realize that Karen's life almost makes the Ingalls and the Waltons seem hip and avant-garde.

I look at Karen's children—who seem unaware that their life-style is the embodiment of rural American values—and admit that they have far more in common with the way I was raised than the way my children, their contemporaries, are growing up. I'm not even sure if that's good or bad—but I am sure that between my life in Glendale and Karen's life in Ventura lies a distance far greater than the sixty-odd miles from my house to hers. Her life is the incarnation of what I was raised to live—what I was raised to believe could and would happen. My mother wished nothing more for me than a loving husband, healthy children, and the joys of catering to their needs while fulfilling my own. Somewhere along the line I missed the boat. It worked for Karen but not for me.

When I get homesick for values that went unquestioned during my childhood, for gentle people and simple pleasures, I pack the kids in our tired old car and we head for Karen's. And just as I knew I would, I return to L.A. feeling much better. That good, warm feeling is becoming a tradition in itself.

I'm not sure if it's her happy marriage, her well-behaved children, or her contentment with her less-than earthshaking existence that makes me wonder if Karen has a gift given to only a few. I know that I don't see much of it in the city. I don't see much of it at my house. And more and more, I see people who wouldn't recognize it if they saw it—much less want a piece of it for their own lives.

What I see at Karen's house is serenity. I see a woman who, even when we were teenagers, knew what she wanted and worked hard to get it and then to keep it intact. I see someone deciding that just because her mother (and my mother) lived a certain way doesn't automatically mean that way is useless or hackneyed or silly. I see a sense of quiet proud tradition at Karen's house, and I think I'll always from time to time want to go back for more: to be reassured that my once-upon-a-time dream may have been just a dream for me, but that in a small house in a small town one family is making that dream come true. When I get the go-go big-city blues, Karen's family and its quiet little home dishes out the best medicine on the market.

They say you can't go home again, and they're right. But for me going to Karen's house is the next best thing.

7

Daydreams and Nightmares

One of my favorite songs from Rodgers and Hammerstein's *The King and I* is "I Have Dreamed." The lilting romantic theme of the song is a gentle and bittersweet melody, just the right tempo for chronicling the never-never land of slow thoughts. My silent visions have spilled from daydreams to nightmares to I hope—I hope—I hope fantasies that sometimes, as all good dreams should, come true.

When I think of my past and the romantic notions that stayed with me throughout my marriage, I involuntarily wince. I see in my slow-motion reveries scenes through the distorted lens of time passed; the focus is at once sharper and clearer than when it happened, yet I find it no easier to comprehend. I see things that I saw—but did not perceive—before, but now they have a backdrop of gigantic question marks: "Why?" and "How?" and "What else?" It is as if the last years of my marriage were a mirage—looking just like the thing I wanted until I got close enough to see that nothing was there.

I clearly remember foursome evenings spent sitting on

the den floor playing games like "Waterworks" amid drinks
and carrot cake and laughter. But I now see all too clearly
that I was far too trusting to have seen the chemistry between the two soon-to-be lovers. Would it still look the
same to me now?

I remember talking with my girl friend—for it always
seemed that my car was in her driveway or her car was in
mine—about our marriages, our children, our dreams, and
our youth. And I wonder now if I was too full of my own
words to pay attention to the message behind hers?

I remember the times with her family—a day at the lake
with her cousins, and her sister who stopped at my house
each day, and the aunt who loved to talk about books—
and I wonder if they choose to forget or remember those
times, now that my husband is married to her?

I remember our kids playing together—in my backyard
and in hers—and I have trouble—as do my children—accepting the reality of their new step-brother, step-sister status.

I remember the water-skiing trips, the meals at her husband's restaurant, the parties at her home and the non-
competitive tennis doubles we played at neighborhood
parks on summer evenings, and I remember the parties they
attended at my home. I remember visits to her parents'
home and drinks around their pool. I remember the hockey
games and the car pool and the favors we did for each other,
and I wonder if my eyes were shut all the time? Did I tell
myself to ignore the smiles and the hello/good-bye kisses
and their close friendship because, just as in a dream, I
hoped that someday I would wake up and it would all be
gone? Did I sleepwalk through a convenient courtship that
let them spend months together, their spouses at their sides,
deciding which way to go? I did, I did, I did.

I remember dyeing Easter eggs together and watching
her kids and my kids so she could go to church with my

husband on Good Friday. I remember Christmas decorations, and front-door wreaths, and the birthday parties for their children and mine. I remember the PTA meetings and the Christmas boutique and the parish cookbook we produced. And most of all I remember feeling the nice feeling you get when a neighbor is more than a neighbor; she is a friend.

And, of course, I also remember the whispered hints that slowly began to drift my way, the small rumblings of shock, amazement, and disappointment that registered with other people before they filtered down to me. I remember.

And now that they are married and everything is legal and fitting and proper, when I see them in my mind's eye, I don't see her in her floor-length wedding gown, nor do I see them with her kids clustered around forming a family that conveniently bears my name. I see them on my couch laughing, or in the backyard at a midsummer eve's picnic, or in my kitchen over coffee and cake. I see them as they were, when each played a big role in my everyday life.

Which is, perhaps, the best explanation for why I don't like to daydream all that much anymore.

8

———⋘⋙———

What I Miss (and Don't Miss) Now That I'm No Longer a Wife

As you have surely gathered by now, I did not seek a divorce. When the papers were served I was as surprised and sad as I'd been when my husband walked out the door. All through the long—too long—separation I'd wondered, not hoped but wondered, if there was still a chance for us to make a go of it as a couple. I thought that his reluctance to start divorce proceedings immediately meant some sort of romantic indecision, some stocktaking of our years together as teenagers, our early married life, our children, our dreams. Perhaps, I'd wonder in moments of optimism, he was so overwhelmed by our past that he just couldn't imagine what his future would be like without me.

So much for my hard-nosed objectivity. I soon learned that his reluctance to file for divorce was based as much on the hope that I'd file out of exasperation (and take the weight of decision off his shoulders) as it was on his tangled feelings about our relationship. Although I helped him through school, in his career, and in his investments (and even in getting to know his new wife), at least I didn't help him file for divorce. Which shows that I can be just as "difficult" as the next person when the situation demands it!

The papers were finally served while I was eating at a neighbor's house. It was just as well that it happened publicly because her comforting words and stiff upper lip helped me retain at least a semblance of dignity at that most distressing time.

Ever since that hot summer night, when I walked home after dinner, with papers announcing my imminent divorcée status clutched in my hand, I've spent a great deal of time thinking about the difference divorce has made in my life. While there are a great many positive aspects to being alone, it's hardly, as you well know, a bed of roses. There are things I positively long for and others to which I have happily bid "good riddance." Every woman has her own list, but here's mine:

I miss the emotional security of just being married; of being "like everybody else." I have trouble shaking the old-fashioned notion that being divorced is somehow unusual or not as acceptable as being married. I know this is an outdated, hackneyed hang-up left over from too many years spent in parochial schools, too many years in the suburbs, and too many years of seeing myself as someone's wife. There was a certain mindless comfort in knowing that once upon a time someone promised to love and cherish me. Being alone means that "someone" has reneged on the promise.

I don't miss my role as cohabitant with a sports fanatic. A certain silent bliss settled over the house after *he* moved out and took his radio and TV broadcasts with him. After years (and years and years and years) of the Bruins, the

Dodgers, the Angels, the Bruins, the Rams, the Lakers, and the Bruins, I feel unspeakably grateful to be able to listen to Vivaldi or Billy Joel whenever I want. I bask in the knowledge that I will never, ever, have to listen to Howard Cosell's voice again. Monday nights are now reserved for "Little House on the Prairie" with my sons; once upon a time they were nothing more than the "clincher" for *his* bank's football pools. I treasure my newfound freedom from having to salve his broken ego or deal with his maniacal fanaticism—depending on whether *his* team won or lost. The loss of a crucial Saturday afternoon game could often ensure a sour Sunday at the hands of our house's armchair quarterback. I can now—hallelujah!—reserve my attention, enthusiasm, and auditory sensitivity for quieter pleasures, and in this sense, at least, I can happily admit that I feel truly liberated!

I miss having my very own someone to share problems with. A someone who, by definition, is compelled to do more than say "too bad," or "tough break," or "that's a shame." I miss having someone in my life who either knows how—or has the interest in my well-being to find someone who does—to fix the garage door, stop the roof from leaking, or repair a dripping faucet. Beyond having someone solve my problems, I miss having someone around who will feel that my problems are his problems too. There are plenty of times when machines break, children misbehave, and creditors clamor for money that I'd give a lot just for a shoulder to cry on and arms to hug me. When I'm too frazzled and frightened to do anything else, it would be nice to have a partner—and I miss no longer having one.

I don't miss being criticized for what I don't feel deserves condemnation. I can now for the first time buy the clothes I want to buy (for me and for my children), stay up as late (or go to bed as early) as I wish, spend money on food or movies or vacations (or whatever) as I please. If I make a mistake these days, the only finger pointing at me will be my own. I don't miss having a patronizing perfectionist who watches and waits for me to do something wrong. When I do things incorrectly now, just as before, I know it—but now I don't have to have someone else dish up a verbal reassessment of my shortcomings. While the freedom of being alone eliminates the "protection" I once had, I still feel that being answerable only to myself is a splendid side effect of being single.

I miss having an extended family. My family, except for my sons, is practically nonexistent. My husband's brothers, sister, and parents were for many years a family I considered my own. Now that I am alone I miss the holiday gatherings, the sense of building tradition, the awareness of creating memories together as a family unit. Even though they have a new daughter-in-law to take my place, I can't help but think that they too probably miss the good times we used to have.

I don't miss feeling that by being alive and breathing I make someone unhappy. It's much easier on my system to feel that no one is in a state of distress just because of me. Living with someone who no longer loves you (or worse, is in love with someone else) is the most distasteful form of self-torture I can image. Now that I am free of his dark cloud of resentment I can honestly say that I revel in my freedom from disapproval; I don't miss the accusations, the recriminations, or the invectives, and I wish I had escaped them long before I did.

I miss feeling that someone (my someone) on the face of the earth was solid, dependable, honorable, and devoted to me. I miss my Rock of Gibraltar who, unfortunately, turned to sand. I miss being able to believe in someone's simultaneous virtue and affection and I miss having a title that shows I'm part of a pair. I miss having someone who, simply because he loves me, is (or at least pretends to be) proud of me and what I do. I miss being able to cling to the high school dreams of living happily ever after and to the handsome knight-in-shining-armor fairy tale that I swallowed hook, line, and sinker. And I miss not being able to think of our time together in the past without cringing at the hurt that was lying in wait.

I miss my naïveté and I miss my innocence. But I don't miss the price I would have had to pay in order to keep them.

9

Are All Noncustodial Fathers Critical? Probably Not.

There are, or so it is rumored, divorces in which the parents manage to agree on practically everything concerning their children's welfare. These people, the legend goes, automatically know who is the better custodial parent, which rules are inviolable, which are not, etc. I would love to meet such a divorced couple—I would love even more to be half of such a terrific twosome. Unfortunately, such is not my fate. I have been cast as the mother who must fight for every inch. Although I don't enjoy fighting for fighting's sake (I've been called "Peace-at-any-price Marilyn" by the friends who know me best), when I believe in something I can pretty well hold my ground.

Last night, my ex brought the boys back home. He had been on another of his bank-financed business-trips-to-the-States, so he invited the boys to spend the weekend with him. As they returned, I was at the door, anxious to ooh and aah over the expensive toys that are an expected part of their father's visits. He stood in the doorway while the suitcase was brought in and the boys unpacked their "Monster Machine" and the R2D2s, and their other goodies. He didn't want to say good-bye and leave and I didn't want to forget the court's restraining order. So we faced each other; me in the kitchen, him on the porch. I did not remind him that he'd brought the boys home twenty minutes late—I was too grateful to have them back with me to be picky. Unfortunately, he wasn't.

The drama began when he began to talk about the children. I was foolishly hoping to hear him say that they looked healthy and happy and handsome (which they did). It would have been foolhardy to have thought that he might say something about the good job I'd done raising them since he's been gone. Instead, the boys and I learned the same sort of thing that we normally learn whenever their father comes to town. It's the sort of lesson I'd just as soon do without.

I learned that he felt my ten-year-old son was entirely too fatherly toward his younger brother. I listened and nodded and wondered if my older son would be that way if his father were still living with us. Probably not.

I learned that my younger son not only (gasp) doesn't have his grace-before-meals completely memorized yet, but he also cannot correctly add certain single-digit numbers. I learned that Greengates, the swank British school where his new wife's children are enrolled, teaches a far more enlightening and disciplined curriculum than the small suburban school my sons attend. I listened and nodded and wondered if he'd ever stopped to think that if he hadn't moved out, our sons would be at Greengates and her kids would still be at the small suburban school our children used to attend together. Probably not.

I learned that my older son seems to have a certain

amount of difficulty when multiplying fractions and that he should be drilled frequently with flash cards. I listened and nodded and reminded myself that I have had the same difficulty for two decades. I thought about how after working and writing and trying to live a quasi-orderly life in the suburbs each day, I'd much rather spend my time with my sons reading *Eloise at the Plaza* or Robert Louis Stevenson than drilling them with math quizzes. I wondered if the bank vice-president on my porch could understand what it's like to raise two sons alone in the city. I decided, probably not.

I learned that my son's sixteen straight 100s on spelling tests and his B-plus over A mythology report weren't really worth a faraway father's enthusiasm. He didn't ask to see the term paper. Almost like a human computer, he acknowledged and processed the information, but last night there was no laudatory print-out for verbal or linguistic skills. I wondered if he knew that he seemed to be far more aware of our shortcomings than of our strengths. Probably not.

I learned of the good grades and perfect progress his stepchildren were making in their new foreign environment and I learned that when my sons go for their summer visit they will be enrolled in summer school to make up for the real or imagined shortcomings of suburban education and a single-mother life-style. I watched the blue-eyed banker as he offered his suggestions about what I could do, in my spare time, to improve my sons' athletic, math, science, deportment, tidiness, and devotional skills. Had someone listened to a tape of his conversation, it might have fostered visions of a father speaking about two ghetto youths in the presence of a down-and-out uninterested mother.

As the "suggestions" quietly continued I looked around

and saw two little boys—not perfect, but certainly adorable—who are loved and wanted and provided for to the
best of my ability. I saw a mother who, although on the
road to postdivorce recovery, was devoting as much time
and interest and care to her sons as was humanly possible. I
saw a nice house in the suburbs festooned with kindergarten art and hockey trophies and probably a surplus of smiling photos of the family who lived there. And I saw a
once-every-other-month weekend father who found it easy
to believe that everything about us could be improved—if
only we'd listen to his sincerely given advice.

After he'd exhausted his rundown of "shoulds" he
turned to leave, gave the boys good-bye kisses, and admitted "They are good boys. . . ."

The headlights of the Mercedes retreated from our
driveway and I wondered if he knew how happy I was that
I wouldn't have to hear his suggestions for at least another
two months. Probably not.

10

---⋘∞⋙---

First Dates and Other Foolishness

I've decided to share with you the drama of my first post-divorce date. For divorcées who still shun males like the plague, it may help to prepare you for what may be waiting. For those of you who remember your reintroduction to the world of "romance" it may remind you that others have suffered the indignities of a sophomoric single—you are not alone. We have had a common baptism—the reimmersion into the waters of singlehood.

My first date was more—and less—than I'd expected. If you consider my awesome lack of experience and savoir-faire with the opposite sex, it may sound less ludicrous. I'd first dated my husband-to-be at sixteen and married him at nineteen; so my past was less than checkered. It was, frankly, pretty dull.

After he fell in love with my girl friend and the two lovebirds obtained their respective divorces, I realized that I was, sooner or later, going to have to look elsewhere for companionship and love and whatever else a sweetheart was supposed to provide. Listening to the tales of my romantically astute girl friends, I grimly decided that I'd get it later instead of sooner. The vignettes I heard about, "afterwork drinks" and "weekends in Frisco," sent me back into my monastic existence. Fourteen months after "he" moved out, an impatient friend insisted that I venture into the jungle of the singles' social scene. She arranged my first date. I wish her such a "first date" at twenty-nine!

He was not a particularly bad fellow. He had been, eight years before, a co-worker at the office where I'd toiled while my then husband and I were in college. I'll call the man Roy. When we'd worked together, as my memory recalled, Roy had been tall, married to a Scandinavian blonde, the father of two children, and hell-bent on being independently wealthy. He was slowly buying small rental properties which would eventually, he was sure, make him an L.A. Diamond Jim Brady. Our mutual friend later told me that Roy's wife had run off with the family dentist and he'd been on his own for a year or so. She arranged the date, told me when to be ready, cautioned that he would, of course, try to get me "in the sack," and then told me to relax and have a good time on my first date. Have a good time, indeed!

When Roy rang the doorbell it seemed that he had inexplicably shrunk and withered. It was hard for me to believe that eight years could do that much damage to a man, but there he was, slumped in front of me, waiting to be invited in the house. My crestfallen feelings were fueled by the realization that, come to think of it, I'd been looking forward to this date. I'd done all the prerequisite plucking and primping and had dressed to look pretty. After all, it had been fourteen months since I'd had a good reason to look pretty. When I stood there in my high heels and dinner dress and saw Roy in his white shoes and rugby shirt I should have had the presence of mind to feign a headache and say good-night. But since I am a fool I excused myself and went upstairs to change. From there the evening went from bad to worse.

Roy had picked a small run-down restaurant with whirling Hungarian dancing girls and inedible food. Over the greasy goulash he told me about his weakness for (and fondness of) tall lithe blondes who love to play tennis. I am a less-than-lithe brunette who hasn't touched a racquet in five years. I immediately began to feel very old, very dumpy, and very undesirable. Then Roy told me how he'd lost his dearly beloved rental properties to his wife in their divorce settlement; how he found it hard to think of things to do with his kids every other weekend; and how the night life at the marina provided him with a ready-made social set. With a wink, he suggested I sell my house in suburbia and move to the west side because, he assured me, I'd never find a man in, of all places, Glendale.

As I sat through the bad food, the silly dancing girls with their tambourines, the chauvinistic talk about blondes and babes, I was engulfed in sadness. I couldn't remember ever feeling that my ex—the man who no longer loved me—had so bored or appalled me on a dinner date. This encounter with Roy, which was supposed to make me quit longing for the man who had left, had accomplished just the opposite. By the time the main course was served I was aching to have my husband back.

Roy finally quit eating the food heaped on his plate and took me home. At the doorstep he was prescient enough not to make a pass. Instead he gave me a John Wayne-like punch on the shoulder and said:

"Welcome to the fun world of singlehood, kid. You're going to bless the day that your old man walked out."

I numbly nodded and watched Roy and his white shoes walk down my driveway. He got in his souped-up car and headed back to the marina. It was an inauspicious introduction to the drama of postdivorce dating, and, as most distasteful introductions, it left me frightened, disoriented, and depressed. So I did what I usually do in times of crisis— I went upstairs and cried.

11

A Dozen-Year Denouement

When I was young and working on the school paper, I used to dream of sending exciting dispatches from exotic places under my by-line: Kuala Lumpur, London, Hong Kong. . . .

I now see that it was a lovely dream, but nothing more. The stories that fan my imagination and catch my interest, now that I am an adult, are far more likely to originate at the local grocery store, the florist, or the cleaners. The locale may not be exciting, but I've learned that the small dramas in my own neighborhood are not without valuable lessons of their own.

A few weeks ago my younger son and I dropped in to pick up some clothes at the cleaners. The middle-aged lady behind the counter has processed my family's clothes for the past five years and has seen a lot of changes. She has seen everything from baby clothes to business suits to Boy Scout uniforms. She has earned my everlasting gratitude by discreetly refraining from noting that my friend Mrs. S., who used the same shop, had suddenly acquired my name and my husband's clothes on her cleaning bill. The nice lady managed somehow to keep our clothes and our names and our pickup and delivery times distinctly separate. As I write about it now I can't help but chuckle over such a trivial matter, but at the time it seemed so important and it was so appreciated.

Through the years, no matter how rushed by irate or busy customers, this woman always took time to give my sons a cheerful greeting and lollipops. Besides her tact and her kindness to my sons, she also has the prettiest blue eyes I've ever seen. You can see I've come to regard the lady behind the counter as more than a proprietor; she's my friend.

When my son and I went to the shop the other Saturday, she commented that she'd been reading some of my articles. Then she smiled and said conspiratorially, "I could hardly wait for you to pick up your cleaning. I wanted to tell you that my own little drama has a really happy ending. Next month, I'm getting married!"

Surprised, I smiled and wished her happiness and she began to share her experience. "You know," she said, "I thought that I'd never have another love. Why, I've been on my own for twelve years, and I guess I'd convinced myself that for a woman my age love and romance and marriage were part of my past. I had five children to raise—four boys and a girl—and so often when they were little I thought how much easier, how much nicer, it would have been to have had a man around the house. I felt guilty that my marriage hadn't worked out—I wanted them to have a 'normal' childhood. It wasn't meant to be, but still somehow they managed to grow up just fine."

After she gathered my clothes and added up my bill I asked how she'd met her fiancé. "Oh," she smiled, "he works just across the street. We've known each other for years but just as friends. Three years ago his wife died, and even though he was lonely he never once asked me out. You see," she laughed, "he thought that the woman at the cleaners wouldn't find him interesting."

"Well, this past Christmas after a lot of hemming and hawing he finally did suggest that we have a date. And we've been seeing each other ever since. I tell you, it's the most natural thing in the world. Now he tells me that he could kick himself for wasting two years of his life trying to work up enough nerve to ask me out."

While she arranged the plastic over my clothes I found myself admiring this woman's glowing happiness. I realized how much else there was to admire about a woman who had worked to keep her spirits up and her family together for over a decade. I couldn't help but identify with her feelings that love and marriage were probably ghosts of a lifetime past; I'd only recently caught myself making the mental transition from "when" I remarry to "if" I remarry. It seems that you don't have to be alone very long at all before the naturalness of coexistence dims and soon it is forgotten. Like the lady at the cleaning shop, single mothers everywhere probably accept stoically that "now" is the time for children and work whereas "then" was the time for romance and intimacy. I couldn't help but agree with her when she said it was a pity that the two stages sometimes have to be separate, not joined, phases of a lifetime.

What cheered me was the fact that women like my soon-to-be-married friend can retain the ability to respond to love—when it finally does come along. And they can do it in spite of earlier rejection, hardship, or fear of choosing the wrong person (again). It was her ability to be receptive to romance that struck me most.

When I was ready to leave she gave my son a cherry-flavored lollipop and told me the wedding date. Then she patted me on the hand and said, "You know all those things that they say about love the second time around?" I nodded. "Well, dear, I want you to know that after all these years, after five fully grown children, it's all there. The bells, the music, the goosebumps, the fluttery feeling—it's all there, hon, every single precious bit of it. And I've never, ever, been happier."

I walked out of the shop thinking, "Now there's a story"; if she had to wait twelve years for her Mr. Right to come along she deserves "every precious bit of it"—she deserves that and a great deal more.

12

---∙⟨∞⟩∙---

Murphy's Law and the "Ex"-Factor

I should have known better. I was beginning to believe that I was ensconced in divorcée heaven. I'd managed to make the house payment (always a big event) and simultaneously pay the telephone, gas, and electric bills. I'd gone grocery shopping and still had enough money in my checking account to replace the hockey stick my son had lost the week before. He had to have it before Saturday's big game; now I'd be able to buy it without worrying whether or not the check would bounce. Trivial things, sure, but for the single parent, small things like gas bills and hockey sticks can break you. I know.

Elsewhere that evening everything seemed delightful, too. One son had brought home an A on a science project (his first A of the school year) and the other had learned—finally!—to print his name. Together we had watched our favorite family show, "The Waltons," and in an uncanny burst of obedience the boys trudged up the stairs to go to bed without one procrastinating murmur.

I'd like to think that some inherent talent at child rearing produces such behavior, but it's probably more realistic that the examples of cooperative children seen on "The Waltons" and "Little House on the Prairie" inspired them to such good behavior. No wonder they're the only shows that the three of us watch religiously together—they with their popcorn and me with my needlepoint.

I could sense that this was an extraordinary Thursday night. I hadn't heard from my ex in several weeks (oh, how I wanted to do something lovely for his employer—transferring "him" out of the country was such a delightful surprise). I hadn't even heard from any of my son's paper-route customers who normally call to compliment or, more often, complain about tardy or sprinkler-sodden newspapers. I couldn't help but feel blessed—nothing unsettling or unhappy or unpleasant had hit for quite some time. Ah, yes, at last I was the master (mistress?) of my fate and all was going to be fine.

After tucking the boys into bed, tidying the kitchen, and figuring out how much was left over from bill paying, I treated myself to a luxurious bubble bath and decided to delve into the stack of unread fashion magazines that would—once and for all—inspire me to anorexia nervosa-like devotion to my long-forgotten diet.

I should have known better.

Right in the middle of an article about the annoying habit women have of unnecessarily and unknowingly saying "I'm sorry," the phone rang. I lunged out of the bathtub, raced into my bedroom blithely dripping on the hardwood floor while I convinced myself that, the way my luck was going, the call was sure to be an editor saying that his magazine couldn't possibly survive another issue without something from me—or maybe it was a powerful New York publisher begging me to commit my experiences to paper for six-figure hardbound, paperback, and movie-rights sales.

Unfortunately, my good luck ran out right then. Peace of mind ended with that phone call. It was my ex. Long distance. A non-English-speaking operator made sure she'd done her job and then got off the line with a sigh of relief. He said hello. I said hello. He said he was flying to the States and would like to see the boys for the weekend and would pick them up Friday at six. He said good-bye. I said good-bye.

Divorced mothers—whether their children see their fathers every week or every year—surely all experience some of the same turmoil I felt that night. A checklist automatically formed in my mind. I had to remember which clothes to pack. I had to include the vitamins, the toothbrushes, etc. Mothers think of the kids' needs and wants to help them forget their own. If I concentrate on which socks to pack with their church clothes I might forget that I miss them when the boys are gone. If I remember to call the hockey coach and tell him that my son won't be here for the big game, I won't have to think of a devious way to make my son see it not as a disappointment but as an adventure. If I remember to put their matching UCLA sweat shirts in the suitcase I can forestall thoughts that this is only one of thousands of good-byes and see-you-laters that I will have to share with my boys in my lifetime.

I try, at times like this, to remind myself that my sons are not going off with Hydra personified. They are leaving with their father: a man I loved for many years, a man I admired and helped and hoped to spend the rest of my life with. That I allowed myself to become so vulnerable, to become so trusting, to become so convinced of his virtue (he was, after all, my *husband*) that only a bitter divorce could shatter my blind belief in his goodness is not his fault; it's mine.

Before I know where the hours have passed, it is Friday

night. The doorbell rings. He says hello, I say hello. The boys greet him with hugs. He places the suitcase on the porch to "inspect" the contents and make sure I haven't forgotten to pack anything. Evidently he forgets that I take care of these boys all the time and know, far better than he ever will, which shirts they like, which socks are favorites, and which sweaters best highlight their blue eyes. But then I guess he, like most departed husbands, has forgotten many things.

The boys kiss me good-bye, my little one reminds me to kiss his teddy bear good-night when I go to bed, and off they go. They walk toward his new car, to stay with him at nothing less than his members-only club.

Barbara Howar wrote about a divorcée in *Making Ends Meet* who admitted that the fear that her children would love her ex more than they would love her had soon been replaced by deeper fears. When I'd read the book I hadn't understood what she meant—but as I stood on the porch waving good-bye I felt that I could have written that line. I worry about them spending time with someone who actively dislikes me. I worry about them being seduced by his money. I worry about them forgetting the values and manners and sensitivities I've tried to instill, and adopting new ones. His values that are in contradiction with the way we live, the way we behave, the way we love. Their backs recede as they head down the driveway with him and I feel an ache inside as I long to keep them with me, or better yet, join the three men who have played such star roles in my life.

Although I know that they will be well fed, well housed, and well loved while they are with their father, I can honestly say I won't feel at ease, totally, until Sunday night when my boys are back home with me again.

13

---···⧓···---

Waiting Out His Wedding Day

I knew it was a long shot because a new person is so often used as a means of escaping from a relationship. The lovers may talk of marriage and the future but there was good reason to doubt that "they" would marry. They did.

The wedding weekend hung over my head like a saber. It wasn't that I wanted my husband back—it wasn't that I envied my girl friend's having wangled an engagement ring out of him. I don't really know why I was depressed unless it was the idea of the seeming unjustness of two people appearing to have "pulled it off"—they had wreaked havoc in the lives of a lot of people—spouses, children, families, and friends—and now they were going to celebrate the fruit of discord.

Somehow it didn't seem right. The elaborate nuptial plans, with the band, the flowers, the food, and the floor-length dresses seemed in bad taste—for more reasons than one. So I decided not to think about it anymore. Like an automaton I had the boys ready for the Friday-night rehearsal dinner and, as I'd been told, handed them over in their white shirts and dress shoes.

The house was eerily quiet when I woke on Saturday morning. My good friend Donna, who knew both of us but loved me, had insisted that I go to her house first thing in the morning. Too depressed to rebel, I did as I was told.

It was a typical L.A. June day—starting off cool and ominous and building to hot and smoggy. We spent the day the way we'd spent countless Saturdays through the years—shopping. I was reticent and Donna was suffering from logorrhea—as if she couldn't find enough words in the day to crowd out the feelings we both kept within.

By the time we'd stopped to eat I knew their wedding was over. It somehow bothered me much less as a fait accompli than it did when it remained a mere possibility. Don't ask why.

I drove home, poured myself a large glass of wine, and stationed myself on the backyard swing. I decided not to think about my "friends" who were dancing at his wedding, and his family who was drinking champagne and laughing. It hurt that people could cheer a couple who seemed oblivious to the fact that their marriage was being constructed on the ashes of earlier, more tender relationships.

As the afternoon wore on I began, bit by bit, to feel better. It was a day that would let me feel good because I could say I "survived." And feel good I did.

My friends—who as you surely know by now are among the best in the world—warned me about many things when they first learned about my divorce. They had alerted me to the dangers of inept money management, lotharios who prey on lonely divorcées, childrearing crises of single mothers, and so many other real and imaginary evils. By the time I'd weathered the courthouse battle and been officially declared divorced, I felt like a professional troubleshooter who could not only foresee but conquer anything my ex-husband might have had up his less than chivalrous sleeve. If custody battles, economic hassles, and courtroom pyrotechnics hadn't altered my basic grasp on optimism, what could?

His remarriage.

As I sat on the swing contemplating the woman whom he'd chosen as my replacement I decided to try never, ever to compare myself with her. A sure-fire way to get unnecessarily depressed would be to think of the things she is that I'm not. Equally pointless and far more confusing would be to list the qualities I had that she didn't. Neither exercise could ever explain why he preferred her to me— because those reasons surely have far more to do with him than with either me or her.

I decided to try to follow Adela Rogers St. Johns's advice and never shuffle the deck of might-have-beens, the "if" deck. It would only raise speculation about the impossible and the inconsequential. I allowed myself one "if" (what if he came back?) , convinced myself that it would have been awful, and then I promised to forget, to the best of my ability, him, her, and what appeared then as the romance of the century. My friends all guaranteed that they would have their fair share of problems. But I knew I couldn't think about that—I should forget about them and concentrate on me.

I thought how lucky I'd been to not be alone on the day of his wedding. I had been forced to take my mind off the reality that there was a new Mrs. Willison. A not-so-good friend might cheerfully join in the celebration of his new marriage, but a true friend would, as so many of mine did, call or write or visit to remind me that they cared. The friend who spent the day with me when my husband remarried—when I was surely at my worst—is the friend I love like a sister.

I knew not to worry that my feelings of sadness might mean I was still carrying the torch for him. I wasn't. One friend had been happily married to her second husband for five years when she learned that her ex was going to remarry, and it still threw her into emotional turmoil. Why?

Maybe because we each (male and female) like to feel that we are irreplaceable.

Maybe because we know we tried our hardest and still failed and now someone else may try only half as hard and succeed.

Maybe because time makes us forget his shortcomings and remember his virtues—virtues she will reap, we think, without having paid the price.

Maybe because even though it didn't work we still invested time and love and hope and emotional energy in that person and now—we are forced to admit—our investment didn't pan out.

I knew I really shouldn't think of these things on his wedding day. What I knew I had to remember is that any man who remarries obviously holds good, warm, and loving memories about living with someone as husband and wife; otherwise he wouldn't be so anxious to try it again. My husband and I may have given each other plenty of headaches, but we didn't take away each other's capacity for romance, hope, or love.

As I sat on the swing I decided that I was going to consider his remarriage a backhanded compliment. As far as I'm concerned, in a roundabout way, that's really what it is.

14

Sometimes Just Coping Is a Delicate Operation

A few years ago I was silly enough to assume that my education was formally completed on college graduation. How untrue! More and more I've come to see my postdivorce existence as a Ph.D. program in emotional survivorship. The class credits are divided among subjects titled: children, money, "him," self-doubt, and other major challenges.

One of my major challenges came last year when my then four-year-old needed an operation. I have finally made the last payment to the surgeon and now, a full year later, I feel capable of talking about my longest day.

I understand from other parents that my son's ailment was not too uncommon. An obstruction was preventing the normal flow of fluid in the ear and little by little he was going deaf. Manners are crucial to an old-fashioned mother like me, and when my sons don't hear something, they know that saying "What?" or "Huh?" will earn a glare and/or a lecture on politesse, courtesy of mom. The frequency of my little one's "pardon me's?" increased during that year. By the time I'd survived the dissolution proceedings and was preparing for my husband's remarriage, it seemed that every hour was sure to bring more "pardon me's." He was beginning to sound like a broken record, and I knew I had to take him to a specialist.

The doctor was concerned about complications: loss of weight, mouth breathing, and chronic snoring. I explained that I was a near-bankrupt divorcée. He nodded as if he'd heard the same lament from every one of his patients. Then he said, "We're going to go ahead with the operation anyway."

It took nearly a month of additional tests, juggled visitation schedules, and realigned vacation days from work before the date could be set. My son "failed" seven out of eight hearing tests. The doctor said that if he removed the tonsils and adenoids while operating on the ears my son would be healthier in no time at all.

The trauma of surgery caught me at a bad time. Only a few weeks before the operation my husband and my girl friend had become man and wife. The divorce proceedings had left me with far less money (and far bigger legal fees) than I'd expected. The Los Angeles summer was hot and smoggy. My spirits were at an all-time low. Had there been no health problem to contend with, I would only have been demoralized; the idea of my four-year-old undergoing surgery made me slump into a state of hopeless depression.

After we had followed the presurgery directions for one week, a good friend who is also our family dentist arrived at 4 A.M. to take us to the hospital. Surgery was scheduled for seven and I'd been told to be there before five. In a trance I kissed my older son good-bye, asked him to say prayers, and carried my pajama-clad little guy to the car.

If we'd had more money, my son could have entered the hospital the night before the operation and stayed the night after. As it was, I felt lucky that the doctor agreed to operate without my having to post a bond. That's why we were up for the predawn patrol. In the struggle between sleep and dollar signs, single mothers know which always wins.

At the hospital I busied myself filling out forms, providing information about weight, height, age, allergies, and whatnot, and finally the three of us settled into the cheerful little room. The first hour went by with my listening to my son-the-patient prattling happily about the cartoon characters on the wall. The second hour we spent watching him slip into semiconsciousness as the tranquilizers took hold. The third hour was heralded by the arrival—all smiles—of my ex, resplendent in banker's business suit and shiny new wedding band.

My son stayed awake long enough to say a few words to his father, and the rest of the hour was spent watching the two men silently wait it out. Occasionally the banker would attempt conversation ("How's your practice?") and the dentist would express his distaste for the man by monosyllabic answers ("Fine"). The ex-wife sat quietly, drinking coffee, wishing a lightning bolt would strike the banker and remove him, forever, from the room, the city, and the rest of her life.

The tension was relieved when the small, sleeping boy was removed from the room. Nurses rolled him to the operating room—each parent gave him a good-luck-I-love-you kiss—and then he disappeared behind swinging doors. The obsequiously polite banker—still smiling—went to his bank, the dentist went home to his family, and the mother went to the waiting room.

An eternity later the surgeon arrived to explain that there had been a few small problems but the child was fine and if he stayed in the hospital for at least eight hours he could go home that night. Limp with relief, the mother, alone in the room, did what any mother would do. She cried.

By 11 A.M. it seemed the day would never end. My boy had been in his room, sporadically sleeping and crying, for two hours. I guess he felt that silence or screams were his only alternatives. At noon his ten-year-old brother arrived. He'd somehow sneaked by the nurses and found the right room. He brought a dozen carnations, a Mickey Mouse puppet, and some candy bars. It was the bright spot of the day. After a quick conversation and plans to meet back home when the day was over, he stealthily returned to his bicycle and his summertime chores.

By four o'clock I was exhausted. Taking advantage of my son's nap periods I sat in the straight-backed chair and began to drift off. I should have known better. I was startled awake by the presence of the banker and his mother-in-law. This woman, whom I had entertained in my home, back when she was my girl-friend's mother, did her best to smile as much as the banker. They each carried a bag of toys for my son and the three of us surrounded the bed—my son unable to talk, only to gesture—until the smiling twosome, not a moment too soon, left. I had tried to prepare myself for the unwelcome, unpredictable presence of the banker. But I had not known he would bring reinforcements from his remarriage.

The day wore on, holding my son and me captive in a recuperative time warp. The surgeon came by in the early evening and said my son would be allowed to go home if I promised to keep him in bed. With grateful promises I prepared to go home, to try to get some sleep, to leave the antiseptic and the nice nurses behind. I bundled up my son and the flowers and the puppet and we headed, via wheelchair, to our car.

When I pulled in the driveway I saw that my good and dear friend JoAnn was at the house. She had decided that I had been out of my mind when I'd refused her earlier offers of postoperative help. She had fresh linens on the bed, dinner on the stove, plenty of punch and ice cream for my son, and a glass of chilled wine for me. I was speechless with surprise and gratitude.

It seemed the day would end without further hassles—my son was resting quietly and I was beginning to feel like a human again—when the doorbell rang. It was my ex. He ingratiatingly asked if he and his wife could come in to visit. By reflex I numbly said, "you can—she can't." It was odd to think that only a few months before—before the hurts—she and I had entered each other's homes without so much as bothering to knock.

His smile and his manners gave way to a withering glance of surprise and disapproval. He couldn't understand why I wasn't happy to see him, why I didn't want to continue my camaraderie with the friend he'd married, why I wouldn't forgive or forget; and I was far too tired to explain. He left his bride sitting in the car while he came in to see his son, offer suggestions about postoperative care, and remind me that his wife was now my son's mother too. I thanked him for his concern and his criticism and quietly said "good-night."

I put the covers around my son, crawled into bed, and finally—amid nightmarish visions of operating tables, changeable husbands, and bankruptcy court—fell asleep. The longest day of my life had ended. The rest of my problems would have to wait until the next day. Only so many challenges could be squeezed into one twenty-four-hour period.

15

Baby-Sitter/Housekeeper/ Housecleaner/Maid

Because some of the details of the travails in my less-than-together life threaten to sound like soap opera, I'm usually reluctant to write about them. To me, the fact that they happen at all signals a small step backward in my life. That I usually survive the upheavals does not ease my discomfort and disappointment.

This tongue-tied reaction to problems surely started with my rather strict education at the hands of nuns who had been sent from Ireland to turn crazed young girls into ladies (or an acceptable facsimile thereof). These women felt that there was only one kind of "problem"—the kind that came from the powers-that-be and were, of course, really blessings in disguise. These included fire, flood, pestilence, and death. The other kind of annoyances, what we secular mortals call problems, were shrugged off as "people piques."

Unfortunately, the bulk of the problems that fill my life these days are delivered at the hands of people. According to the hands that rocked the cradle of my adolescence, these intrusions were to be overcome or overlooked.

I was raised to believe that if one had the misfortune to have problems with people, the solution consisted simply of learning what the situation required and then slowly untangling the anger or hurt or dislike so that all parties could walk arm in arm into the sunset. No wonder I try to pretend that people problems don't cloud my life—it's such a distasteful admission of failure.

If I'd learned my girls' school lessons well, my little guilt-ridden voice reminds me, I wouldn't have personality problems to overcome in the first place. Everyone would, the cherubic voice of Sister Mary Consolata intones, want nothing more than to be my ally and friend—it was just a matter of learning how to adapt.

So, it's with a great deal of reluctance that I admit that a problem with my baby-sitter has been a part of my post-divorce existence. Our baby-sitter has many names—she sees herself as the housekeeper because she genuinely believes the house is hers, not mine. Consequently, she runs it as if she owned it. Niches where I stow socks or towels or hair curlers become depositories for her possessions—my goodies disappear into crevices that are discovered days, weeks, or months later as the new home for bed linens, pantyhose, or hockey equipment. Because I can't work without someone in the house to supervise afterschool youngsters, I willingly let the "housekeeper" get away with whatever she wants in hopes of ensuring her willingness to stay. This has been going on for years.

Since I call this divinely essential woman a baby-sitter and she calls herself a housekeeper, you should know that my five-year-old son calls her the housecleaner. He does this because she is tolerant of his many idiosyncrasies, with the exception of his rather intense love affair with dirt. I've been told that little boys are, by nature, less than pristine. But my perpetually cheerful young man possesses a rare genius for fingermarks, spills, foot tracks on carpet, and cookie-crumb trails. It is no wonder he sees the woman with whom he spends his afternoons as the house "cleaner." So now that we know this woman is really the baby-sitter/housekeeper/housecleaner—her importance staggers the mind.

My ex-husband, who, several years ago, couldn't understand why I wasn't overly enthusiastic about juggling one husband, two little boys, a full-time office job, writing assignments, and housekeeping-cum-laundry (during my spare time), reluctantly agreed to hire a housekeeper since, after all, someone had to be home in the afternoons. Without my paycheck, it was reasoned, there'd be no house for the kids to come home to, so we hired help. That was several years ago; the only thing that has changed is the no-longer-present husband.

One of the clearest memories of my otherwise hazy marathon divorce proceedings was his sarcastic accusation from the witness stand that I had (gasp) a "maid." Since she had been interchangeably referred to as the "baby-sitter" and "housekeeper" for the first two days of the proceedings, I could imagine the judge visualizing our little, less-than-wealthy family with a retinue of uniformed women hovering around us à la "Upstairs, Downstairs." I still smirk at my ex's outrageous remark that the willful baby-sitter/housekeeper/housecleaner is (harrumph) a "maid." Anyone with a brain in his or her head knows that single mothers don't need maids—we need resourceful, encouraging, dependable jacks-of-all-trades. And we probably need them even more than we need husbands.

At any rate, this woman resides at the epicenter of my family's existence. She supervises everything: what I buy at the grocery store, what my son wears to kindergarten, when I can or cannot conveniently take a vacation day.

On Friday night several months ago, as I was paying her, the baby-sitter/housekeeper/housecleaner/maid hinted that she really needed to earn more money. She asked if I had any ideas. I assured her that I would think about the problem (knowing full well that I couldn't come up with any more cash) and I wished her a nice weekend. The next morning a friend and neighbor telephoned to say that she couldn't keep her house as clean as her husband wanted—would I ask our lady if she'd like to work one day a week at her house across the street? Idea! I asked around and found yet another friend who wanted a little help with housework, so my house became a mini-dispatch station. Our housekeeper worked for us three days a week; the remaining two days she worked for my friends. The plan went well—everyone was happy—and the "maid" was earning almost more net income than I.

The problem came on a Friday morning when she called and said she could not come to work—she was ill. Her sister-in-law would drive her over in the evening to pick up her week's salary. I called my office, explained that I had to stay home, and mentally switched gears from breadwinner to bread baker. I told myself she would be back on Monday morning and a day away from deadlines and temperamental supervisors would do me good.

I never saw our housekeeper again, which is why I'm writing this. It was a shock to my system to wake up on Monday, get dressed, and wait—and wait and wait and wait—for her arrival. It took two hours before I realized I'd been fired as an employer. Through her friends I later heard that someone in Santa Monica had hired her to do for their family what she did for mine—but at a salary substantially higher than what my friends and I together were paying. So now the baby-sitter/housekeeper/housecleaner/maid really does earn more than I do. So much for the earning power of my college degree.

I've got to find someone fast to take away the ever-growing list of "can'ts" that are beginning to dominate my life. I can't go to work without someone around to walk my little one back and forth to the neighborhood kindergarten. I can't think of good excuses—or a good replacement—for my two friends who also depended on the housekeeper's help. I can't find where the iron and the electric curlers and the Windex have been hidden. I can't continue to buff floors and polish silver and wash dishes while my boss fumes over my absentee record and my editors wonder about past-due deadlines. Most of all, I can't imagine someone not wanting to stay with my family. Just as in a divorce, I find myself wondering what the family in Santa Monica could possibly have that we don't have. I can't think of a thing—except, of course, money.

16

Valentine's Day

I might as well confess to you that, in spite of the emotional bumps and bruises I've weathered over the past thirty years, I'm an incurable, hopeless romantic. This affliction, in a cycle that is comparable to that of hay fever, resurfaces every February without fail. Since red roses, lace, and perfume do powerful things to me, you can probably imagine what happens each Valentine's Day. I'm a mass of quivering, mushy sentimentality. I keep waiting to outgrow such silliness. So far it hasn't happened.

While some of my friends go for big (i.e., expensive) gifts, I can easily be moved to speechless rapture over a flower or a handkerchief or even a handwritten poem. I still think I fell in love with my ex-husband because he was not only romantic enough to write poems to me in high school but brave enough to pass them to me during classroom lectures. Such chivalry was particularly effective for the starry-eyed schoolgirl I was when we met.

I grew up, as did many women of my generation, with visions of Prince Charming, romantic ballads, and happily-ever-afters. Today I don't believe in those things any more than I believe in fairy tales, but they're still appealing reminders of the girl I used to be, and the dreams I used to dream.

I haven't had a valentine, an honest-to-goodness valentine, for quite some time. But I've saved the last gift I received on a not-too-distant February 14. It was from my husband—my then husband. He gave me a bottle of perfume and a card. On the front of the card was a close-up photograph of a woman's hand holding a long-stemmed red rose. She was gently pressing the flower to her heart and she was wearing a white ruffled silk blouse. You could see the blouse, the hand, and the rose, but you could see neither face, nor body, nor background. I don't know who was holding the rose but now I realize it certainly wasn't me.

Don't ask me why I've kept the card—I don't have a good answer. Everything else that might remind me of my decade-long delusion has been tossed out. The two closets full of clothes he left behind were given to the needy; the doodads and gifts from high school were discarded in a fit of spring housecleaning; and the jewelry he gave me, wedding ring and all, was sold to pay for hockey lessons, doctor's bills, and property taxes. The only things I've kept are the lace-tied bundles of teenage love letters and the Valentine's Day card with the picture of the rose and the faceless female.

Perhaps I need to have proof that someone once was in love with me. Or maybe I want to return to those long-ignored letters when I'm white-haired and wrinkled in order to be able to recall my youth and my high-school sweetheart. Or maybe I'm just a mindless masochist.

Most probably, the Valentine's Day card and the stacks of love letters stay in my possession to remind me and remind me and remind me that "nothing is forever." When people fall in love or stay in love it doesn't mean that sentiment will not, cannot, be sabotaged, eroded, or killed.

I think about that when I look at the card. I know by heart what he wrote on the inside. It said, "Dearest Marilyn, Because I love and want you as much today as I did ten years ago . . . Your Valentine."

I also know by heart that it was about a month after he gave me the perfume and the card that he told me he was going to move out.

Maybe the girl I used to be and the dreams I used to dream lie dormant all year. And then each February 14 they resurface to try to teach me a lesson about the transitory nature of flowers and perfume and Prince Charmings.

And still, and still, each Valentine's Day I find myself wanting very much to believe in happily-ever-afters. Maybe we all do. . . .

17

———◦∞◦———

Vignettes from the Life of a Would-Be Very Famous Writer

Here are a few vignettes from the life of a divorced mother trying to make her mark.

When I was a little girl my parents kept telling me to try with all my might and to believe in myself. So I emerged from childhood with the firm belief that there wasn't anything I couldn't do as long as I worked hard and remained confident.

I chose to be a very famous writer. Little did I know. . . .

A trip to New York is planned. It's become apparent that if I'm going to get a book published and if I'm going to land those much-needed extra magazine assignments (one son will need braces, and braces weren't part of my divorce settlement . . .), then I'd better go back east and talk to some Very Important People. I convince myself that it's the *only* logical thing to do. After I get permission slips from my boss, my car pool, and my housekeeper, I call the airline to make reservations. I ask the ticket lady if it's really true that during the airline's special offer my son can fly with me free. She says yes, so I say yes, and grin in anticipation of his delight.

I excitedly call a friend to tell her about my plans for the trip and she says, "Oh dear, that may not be such a good idea. If you make the trip alone you can see so many more people and make far more contacts than you can with a ten-year-old tagging along. You really should think about leaving him home." I hang up the phone, ignore her advice, and start making a list of the clothes I should pack for my son. Maybe I won't be a very famous writer after all. . . .

I mail an article to a well-known women's magazine. They can't help but love it, I tell myself, and if they buy it, I can get my son a new suit for the trip to New York. As it is, I can't afford the trip, much less the suit, but I'm always sure something will turn up to bail me out. I call the magazine editor on Monday and Wednesday and Friday. The first time I learn that the original editor has been promoted so I'll have to talk to someone else. The next call lets me know that the new editor is out of town. The third time I'm put on hold for ten minutes while his secretary tries to locate him "just around the corner."

She finally picks up the phone and breathlessly admits that she really can't figure out where he is. Sensing my disappointment, she does tell me that my article is being passed around because "they" can't decide whether to buy it. If I call next week, she tells me, they may be closer to making a decision. I decide not to call that editor any more—my phone bill has already taken too big a bite out of the profit from a sale of the article. I'll just let fate take its course—let the editor call me. Maybe I won't be a very famous writer after all. . . .

A New York publisher has sent me a letter suggesting

that I write a book about divorce. Overflowing with optimism, I work night and day until I have two chapters completed. I bundle them up and nervously send them to the Very Important Publisher who will make me rich and famous. He'd better.

I call him and offer to see him while I'm in New York on the trip I can't afford. His secretary listens patiently while I give my name, the title of my book, and the subtle reminder that I'm calling all the way from California. In a voice that would do any haughty dowager proud, she icily harrumphs, "You should know, Ms. Willison, that Mr. VeryImportantPublisher *never* speaks to authors." Taken aback, I fumble for some way to escape the stigma of being a writer. Rendered speechless by intimidation I decide that maybe I won't be a very famous writer after all. . . .

During the drizzly month of March, I am working on a book review to be printed by the *Wall Street Journal*. The publicity agent for the book has assured the reviewers that it won't be published until the beginning of May, so there is no desperate need to shape up my disconnected scribbles and scrawls until the end of April. As long as the review is published the same week as the book goes on sale, all will be well. While shopping for an April Fool's gag gift I see the book I'm supposed to be reviewing displayed prominently in a bookstore window! In a panic, I rush home, give the boys a quick kiss, and hug and explain my predicament. I hurriedly tell them that as soon as my review is typed I'll come out of seclusion. Then I sequester myself in my bedroom and try to get the review ready before the mailman arrives. Just when I think I may salvage the whole deal, the phone rings. The call must be for my son since no one calls me to the phone, so I keep typing.

Just as I'm working on the last page my son knocks on

the bedroom door and says he absolutely has to talk to me. Before I can ask him to wait, he walks in with tears in his eyes and tells me he won't be able to play on the neighborhood baseball team. The coach had called to say that this year there were just too many applicants; if he tried out next year he might be able to make the team then. I can smell a crisis brewing and it's obvious that my boy is deeply disappointed and in need of mothering. Wishing I were capable of twitching my nose so my son could be on the team, but knowing that's only for TV sitcoms, I turn off the typewriter, wipe away his tears, and suggest that we talk about this problem over a bowl of ice cream. We leave the book and the review and the typewriter and head for the kitchen. Maybe I won't be a very famous writer after all. . . .

I am turning in an article to a famous Mild-Mannered Newspaper Editor. Because I'm somewhat unsure about the controversial slant of my article (it's extralong, too) I quickly leave his office. On my way out I recognize one of my favorite Very Famous Writers. She is smiling, cheerful, and surprisingly nice to me. I tell her which of her books and articles I've particularly liked and she (surprise! surprise!) comments about which of my newspaper columns she has liked. She gives me her advice for dealing with cranky publishers, critical editors, and crucial deadlines. We talk for half an hour nonstop about our projects and our children and our dreams. After she gives me her East Coast address and phone number and I give her my West Coast ones, I drive home feeling like a very fortunate fourth grader.

The Very Famous Writer unknowingly reminded me that my parents may have been right. Maybe I will be a very famous writer after all. . . .

18

---❧---

Biting the Bullet
for Baseball

I am now going to confess to you that I was never meant
to be the mother of sons. I felt, nay, believed, that my
offspring would be female. With each pregnancy I would
rest my hand on my rotund middle and daydream of the
little girl to whom I would teach grands jetés and pirou-
ettes. I fantasized about matching lacy mother-daughter
sleepwear sets, and of teaching a daughter the intricacies,
the skills my mother taught me. All that daydreaming
became a waste of time when I was given—hallelujah!—
two red-blooded, all-American boys. And I've been learning about "men" since the day they were born.

Spring has brought me a new awareness this year—my
hockey-playing ten-year-old has just been "drafted" by a
neighborhood baseball team. The house is strewn with
Gloveoleum, bats, cleats, and mitts. Names like Rogie
Vachon and Marcel Dionne have been replaced with
Tommy John, Steve Garvey, and Hank Aaron. When I
arrive home after work I no longer see a puck and a street-
hockey stick blocking my path to the garage—now there's
a barricade of baseball bats.

This might not be cause for alarm if I were a normal mother. I am not normal, you see. This woman who was once an eighth-grade cheerleader is, in fact, chronically allergic to sports.

This ailment has plagued me since childhood. I was raised in a home that functioned on the belief that idle hands were the devil's workshop. To watch someone do anything was a poor and unacceptable substitute for doing something yourself. When my mother was tired or worried or depressed she did not sit and brood—she baked. When my father was upset over the stock market or perturbed with a co-worker, he would garden, build something, or seek the sanctuary of his tool-shed-cum-garage in search of a job.

Games were not a part of my family's existence because one needed something tangible to show for one's time—a cake, a new sweater, a repainted trellis, a refinished chair—something! The only "sport" I can remember at home on TV was the Friday night fights during the fifties. When I asked Mama why Daddy watched them she shrugged her shoulders and said, "Because he likes Jack London's books." It took years before it dawned on me how important boxing was in London's writing.

When my son showed interest in hockey I was delighted. I reasoned that even though it was (shudder) a sport, it was the perfect way to acquire a new skill—ice skating. The standard sports, it seemed, required nothing more complicated than standing, walking, or running while wearing whatever uniform the pastime dictated. And while I was not about to play football with my son, I gladly drove to the ice rink to skate with him and discuss preadolescent problems while we worked on turns. I couldn't imagine a good mother-son talk in the midst of dunk shots, tackles, or home runs.

But now this Little League thing has erupted and I am stuck. The idea of watching a baseball game sets my teeth on edge—even though I'll see my son imitate Mickey Mantle or Mr. Coffee. Already I am preparing my "Little League lunchbox"—I've got needlework, crossword puzzles, and paperback books gathered to take to the games. I can envision a sunburned, sweaty me watching a dusty, determined him. He will approach home plate confident that his mother is in the stands cheering him toward victory. Unaware that I am sitting there developing willpower and discipline, he'll hit a home run and we'll return home to celebrate with milk and cookies.

Surely, I wail, I am not alone. Surely there are other women who dearly love their sons but are unable to generate more than mock enthusiasm for pursuits they neither understand nor enjoy. I can barely sit through a full meal without fidgeting—a nine-inning game will stretch before me like an eternity, all nonproductive. At least with the hockey games I could criticize skating skills. Who can criticize how someone stands in left field?

I envy mothers who can sit contentedly and enjoy watching their lives tick away at their sons' baseball, football, and basketball games. I've decided to watch these women closely and see how they acquire that serene look. My son has just informed me that "we" have about forty baseball games this season. As soon as I recover from the shock, I'm sure I'll find something suitably enthusiastic to say. At this point, I'm busy praying that my allergy to sports will, in time, go away. It's going to have to because Little League will outlive me.

19

Horror Stories I Have Heard

The worst thing, I've decided, about being a divorcée is that there is no panacea for the tumult of problems that arise. Adela Rogers St. Johns, whom I more than admire—I venerate—quoted in one of her books a man who told her that humans would be better able to cope with misfortune if it marched up, introduced itself, and then dished out the bad stuff. Instead, misfortune sneaks up behind you when you least expect it, clobbers you over the head with a two-by-four, and then keeps pelting you once you're down to make sure you don't get back on your feet a moment too soon.

That's exactly how I see divorce. It comes when you least expect it. It hands out an overdose of heartache and then—as if that's not enough—when you are at your weakest, it gives you a series of headaches labeled money; children who can't understand why their daddy (or mommy) moved away; ex-spouses who seem to see their total purpose in life as the reopening of deep wounds; and loneliness and self-doubt. Any one of the problems alone would be major—combined, as they are in divorce, the odds are powerfully against you.

On blustery, dark days, in spite of my adorable children, my wonderful friends, my writing, and my inbred optimism, I sometimes get more than a little discouraged. That's when I try to console myself with the fact that my personal horror story is one of many that happen in Los Angeles every year.

Sometimes it can be helpful to know that however unpleasant your divorce experience was or is, there's always someone around the corner who can match it, blow for blow, and still have some left over. Here are a few vignettes for you—I've decided to collect them as "Horror Stories I have Heard."

The first is about a man named Bob. Bob works for a large bank. In spite of a great deal of effort, he and his wife couldn't make a go of their marriage. After several off-again-on-again attempts they separated for good—he to a new home in the desert, she to her parents' home. It didn't take Bob long to realize that he was much happier without the constant squabbling and hurts that had dominated their brief marriage. Deciding to do what had to be done, he took a day off work and drove from his home to the city where his wife was living with her parents.

He met with her and tried to convince her that they were each happier away from the other. He told her that his new home was a source of solace for him—that he had merged their furniture with the antiques he'd collected during his travels before their marriage and established a comfortable bachelor home in a hot climate. He gave her a set of house keys and suggested that she go to his place the following week and retrieve whatever furniture and other things that she wanted from the marriage—to make things easier for her, he would stay at his office during the day so that she wouldn't have to go through the tearful division of property.

Bob slowly walked back to his car (a long-ago injury and a need for special shoes made it impossible for him to hurry) and decided to do what most men do when their personal lives are a disappointment—he threw himself into his work.

After the appointed property-division day was over, Bob reluctantly returned to his desert home. What he saw was a scene out of a mystery movie—everything, *everything*, had been taken from the house. His collection of antiques, his memorabilia from his teenage trips to the Orient, pictures, dishes, pans, silverware, linens, everything. He went from room to room, but to no avail. The final blow was finding his custom-made suits cut in strips and stuffed in the fireplace, and seeing that all his special shoes—the only kind he could wear—had been taken, along with his underwear, along with everything he'd owned. Bob is more successful than ever in his business, but the mere mention of marriage gives him a bad case of the hives, and who can blame him?

Now here's the lovely girl of twenty who met a man almost a decade her senior. He was a widower with four little children. After his wife's death he was lost—desperate about being alone, terrified at the prospect of raising preschoolers. He persuaded Miss J., after a whirlwind courtship, that he couldn't live without her—he needed her, the kids needed her, etc. They married and she moved into his house and devoted herself to being what she'd always wanted to be, a full-time homemaker and mommy, for six years. They were hectic, hardworking years, but she was where she'd always wanted to be—with people who needed her.

The roof fell in when her husband let her know that he was in love with a woman at his office and that his new lady was going to divorce her husband and the two planned to marry as soon as possible. Our young friend, Miss J., was told to move out; after all, it wasn't her house. Now she's trying to carve out a new life for herself.

For the first time she's living alone and she desperately misses the kids. "I feel as if I had a six-year stint as live-in help. I learned to love them, to help them, and be a part of their lives. I wound up with no house, no kids—nothing. Nothing except memories."

Or how about Pete? Pete is a thirty-three-year-old survivor of two unpleasant divorces. He's a kind, gentle man with a delicate, doe-eyed look. Either he is fatally attracted to beautiful, unscrupulous women, or else they see him coming and set ingenious traps.

His second wife's departure left Pete in a state of shock— we think he'll recover but we're taking bets that the next woman he falls for will be very, very plain.

Pete's ex was the apple of his eye. Although he was somewhat frail and phlegmatic, she was bouncy and gregarious and full of energy. He would watch her dance or play tennis and comment to us on how lucky he was to have such a beautiful, active wife. He admitted that she spent a small fortune on clothes and, yes, the new sports car she bought was expensive, but an extravagant, beautiful wife seemed much better to Pete than the thrifty loneliness he'd known before their marriage.

For their anniversary last December, Pete and his wife took a trip to the Bahamas at her urging. While there he agreed to buy the ring and necklace she "just had to have." He also paid for a lot of clothes during the trip—but he didn't find out about them until the charge-account statements came later. One week after they returned from their vacation, Pete came home from work to an empty house. His wife had taken the jewelry and the clothes and the sports car—leaving Pete with divorce papers and gargantuan bills. She moved in with her new boyfriend while Pete sat in their Christmas-decorated house wondering when she might return. Of course, she never did.

The next horror story is about a woman named Barb. Barb has the indelible stamp of "loser" across her face and things just seem to go from bad to worse in her life. She is fifty, works as a secretary for a big company, and looks sixty-five on bad days. She's been having a lot of bad days lately.

Barb is a chain smoker. The nicotine has worked its wonders on her skin and hair and hands. She's not at all pretty but if you look closely you can see that once she must have been a fragile-looking girl with pretty blue eyes and a slender figure. Now you see a slightly stooped, poorly dressed woman who looks frightened all the time.

Barb was married for several years but her husband was less than gentlemanly. She was left with a young son who learned from his father's example to terrify Barb the way his father had done. The son is no longer young and he bullies Barb whenever he isn't in juvenile court. He has stolen her car, he has beaten her, he has made her life a nightmare, a living reminder of a sour marriage.

Last month Barb missed a week of work because of her bruises and black eye, courtesy of her son. Her friends are wondering what it will take for Barb to learn that people only bully those who let themselves be abused. They also know that it's too late for Barb to learn a lesson she should have learned twenty years ago.

And then there's Nancy. Nancy was married for a decade to a very successful stockbroker—they hadn't had any children, which disappointed them, but they had a good marriage anyway. When Nancy turned thirty-seven she discovered that she was pregnant. It was the nicest surprise she and her husband had ever had—and by the time she was forty-one she'd had two more such surprises.

Nancy was finally living a dream come true, until she woke up to the nightmare of a husband who no longer loved her—he didn't know if it was because of the three kids who disrupted their life together; or that Nancy now seemed so dowdy; or that he wanted to have fun, and it was hard to have fun with so many responsibilities. At any rate, he moved out.

Nancy now has three preschoolers, no job skills, and no husband: "He whizzes by the house to visit the kids, jumps out of his sports car, dashes in the house wearing jogging outfits and tennis clothes. He can't seem to understand that we desperately need money—children are expensive to care for. But he's too busy with aerobic exercises to get the point. Raising three little ones is a big job for someone in her twenties—for someone my age it is herculean. I'd like to wrap that damn tennis racquet, the sixty-dollar one, right around his neck."

The next horror story is about the movie star and the stunt man. The movie star was married to a quiet, mousy man, the father of her little son. Her career was going up, up, up, while his was going nowhere. On the set one day she fell under the spell of the tall, handsome, suave stunt man who was deeply attracted to horses and women (in that order). The movie star divorced her husband, married the stunt man, and they set up housekeeping on a large ten-acre ranch. He handled the earnings from her films and tried to turn her small son into a miniature man.

Their marriage seemed to satisfy them—she had her name alongside those of leading stars, and he had to do fewer and fewer stunts. His time was occupied with horses and the ranch and other women. While she was at the studio and her son was at the very expensive private school, the stunt man had time on his hands, and lots of money in the bank, to do whatever pleased him. They were, as far as the public was concerned, the perfect couple—she was sultry and earthy and he was sophisticated and elegant.

One day, as the limousine waited in the circular driveway, she kissed her sleeping husband and little boy goodbye. The maid handed her her coat and she went to the studio as on any other day. The quiet auto descended into the city, leaving the stables, the orange groves, the garden, the four cars, the servants' quarters, the tractor, the pool, the tennis courts, and the family behind. When the day was over, she returned and found that everything movable was gone. Her son was waiting on the doorstep, locked out. There were no cars, no servants, no horses—even the hay was gone!

A lesser woman might have killed herself or gone beserk or killed the stunt man. But this woman did what movie stars are trained to do—she called her agent and together they contacted Melvin Belli. But that's another story. She later found out that half an hour after she left in the limousine, five big moving vans had rolled up. The servants had been fired, the utilities had been turned off, and the working ranch had come to a standstill in one working day.

And the movie star? She's still with us, although she avoids the film industry like the plague, and every now and then, in her little house in suburbia, she can be heard humming her favorite song, "What a difference a day makes, twenty-four little hours. . . ."

I no longer look at people the way I used to. Now when I see pedestrians or sports fans or office workers I see them as Miss. J. or Pete or Nancy, each with a story to tell.

Each person out there in the big city, I'm learning, holds a very personal horror story. The moving force in the plot may be illness or divorce or death—but it's a horror story nonetheless. It may center on disappointing children, demanding parents, bosses who yell, or co-workers who condemn. Like the skeleton in the closet, the horror is known, if at all, to only a few. Unlike a scar or a blemish, it is not visible. But I think we each have a skeleton hanging somewhere.

Maybe the not-so-nice parts of being human are hardest to accept because they're so essential to growth. What's underneath a scab isn't going to get better unless there's a little ugliness. I see nothing wrong with admitting that every life takes a few wrong turns and runs into mistakes. Maybe we can learn that a stumbling block is only a postponement—whether or not it turns into a dead end is no one's decision except our own. Maybe the value of horror stories is that we can learn that other people have dealt with misfortune's two-by-four—just as we had to—and have survived to talk about it.

20

Thanksgiving Memories

Although my Thanksgivings are unwaveringly enjoyable, I know that many people spend the holiday much as described in one of my best-remembered *New Yorker* magazine "Talk of the Town" columns: a mixture of football, family rivalries, and starchy food. Fortunately, for me and my boys Thanksgivings are the same each year. Reliable, traditional, a source of wonder that one thing, one holiday, can remain the same in spite of changing life-styles.

I'd like to share one with you.

We begin the preparation for the holiday on Tuesday night. That's when the clothes must be packed for our annual trek to my cousin's house. My cousin, who is as dear to me as a sister would be, is the only person I now know who knew me when I was a child. She has seen me through all the gawky and inexplicable stages of childhood, adolescence, and now womanhood—and let me know that she has loved me no matter what. She is one of the few people I would adore having as a next-door neighbor; unfortunately, she lives four hours from Los Angeles and our visits are restricted to vacations or holidays. I tell you all of this to explain why I get so excited about the holiday, why I can hardly wait to arrive at her house, why I always know what it will be like.

My cousin and her husband live at the base of the Sequoias in a small community of winding roads, tall (and I mean really tall) pine trees, streams, deer, squirrels, clear air, and starry skies. A visit to her house is like a week in camp for my boys. They run out of the car and dash into the cabin to announce our arrival before I can turn off the ignition. It's as if they feel as much at home at her house as I do.

On Tuesday night the oldest, dirtiest clothes are gathered for us to wear while in the mountains. Not that we're perfectly organized. Invariably I leave something crucial behind each year. This time I forgot the sleeping bags, last year the toothbrushes. Travel gear is grouped in the middle of the boys' room. The children have a hard time getting to sleep because there is an air of expectation in the house—but not of pending surprise as at Christmas. This is Thanksgiving at Terry's and we all know what's in store.

There's a sense of urgency—to stop wasting time and get where we must go so we can start enjoying ourselves. When we wake on Wednesday morning we have the same excited, happy feeling. We make a three-way pact to hurry home as fast as possible so we can get to the mountains before everyone has gone to sleep. Even as we say it we know it's a joke—Terry and her family would wait up for us until dawn if they had to. We know inside that they are as eager to see us as we are to see them. The boys leave for school and I for work, silently counting the hours until we can join the exodus of cars leaving the city.

When we finally arrive in the mountains—usually around 11 P.M. on Wednesday, the boys are predictably aghast at the number of stars in the sky and the fact that they seem so much bigger and brighter than at home. They don't remember that there's no smog in the mountains.

Before we know it, we're in the house surrounded by people offering hugs and kisses, welcoming us with stories and questions. We sit around the huge fireplace and drink hot apple cider and eat Terry's homemade pie and fresh cookies. Before long, the tired people, one by one, leave to get some sleep. We really need it.

Terry and I are usually the first awake each Thanksgiving. Although I feel practically drunk with power in my own kitchen, I know that in hers I would only be under foot, so I sit and watch while she prepares the feast to be. Soon several hungry people clamor for breakfast: some want cereal, some want rolls, some want bacon and eggs, and all the adults seem desperately to need coffee. Within an hour or two the house is full of talkative—very talkative—people who love each other and are happy to be together, dear to each other, trustworthy, and gentle.

By this time the boys are fishing in the backyard stream. They're also already dirty and cold and wet, but for this one day neither they nor I worry about conditions that back home would be cause for complaint. Today they are happy and free—neither they nor I could want for anything more—or less.

By noon the kitchen is going full blast. Dinner will be served no later than two so that the boys and I can leave by four. There isn't a wasted moment. Soon the children— all six of them—are seated at one table and the dozen or so adults at another. There is an impromptu blessing given by Terry's husband, and then the meal begins. I've eaten the same Thanksgiving menu at least two dozen times, but each year it seems better, tastier, more precious. A different menu wouldn't be Thanksgiving to me. It might be a wonderful meal, but it wouldn't be what I want and need and drive four hours to get—a sense of permanence, of personal and family history, of tradition in my life.

All too soon the clothes have been repacked, the boys are clean and full and tired. I have taken my postmince-meat-pie walk with Terry's son—once my bitter childhood enemy, now my valued and loved cousin—along the windy pinecone-strewn roads. I have tried to use every moment to soak up the feelings that this mountain holds for me so that when I am in my own home, alone and at odds, I will be able to call on the reserves I have stored during this visit. It is never enough but always much better than nothing.

The ten or fifteen people gathered at Terry's house for the weekend feel sorry for me because I must return to the city and go to work the next day. To their way of thinking, nothing is worth leaving the mountain for—especially on a holiday weekend. They see Los Angeles as the true center of dirty air and low living and I can almost hear them asking, "Why does she continue to live there?" After a weekend with Terry and her neighbors I wonder if I'd ask myself the same question.

Before we're off the mountain, the boys have drifted off to sleep. My older son promised to stay awake to make sure I wouldn't fall asleep at the wheel. His protective instincts were in the right place but his flesh, like everyone else's, was weak. Driving along the dark roads, I pray that I'll be able to make it home safely. The two snoring angels in the seat beside me remind me that Thanksgiving doesn't have to be on the mountain with Terry; it doesn't really have to have an abundance of food. It can be in a very old and feeble car on an unlit mountain road with a single mother and two sleeping boys.

Four hours later I pull into the driveway at home. I

tell myself that the car will never make that trip another year. I tell myself that I should think about taking it easy and stop trying to provide the boys with fairy-tale holidays. I tell myself that I'm a crazy lady to do an eight-hour driving marathon when I have to get up and go to work the next day. I carry the boys and their belongings into the house—get them out of their clothes and into their pajamas and tuck them into bed.

Physically I'm in Los Angeles; mentally I'm back on the mountain. I know next year I'll do the same thing all over again. It's what I (and my sons) have come to expect so we can feel the essence of Thanksgiving. But as I close the bedroom door and see my two sleepers, I am forced to admit that perhaps I've been wrong. My Thanksgiving is with me when I am with my sons—when I know that I have people—near or far—who love us, and when I know that being divorced during the holidays is not the worst possible fate.

Being unable to feel that there is something to give thanks for—that's the worst. If little else, my boys and I have been spared that.

21

---∙∙⟨∞⟩∙∙---

Keeping a Car in the Family

My car died last month, which is very sad. That car represented the first major purchase my husband and I made after we graduated from college. Our first car was a relic purchased with the money from the postmarital sale of my little red Austin Healey. Our old, sedate little VW represented the big step from "college kids" to "young marrieds"—the insurance-rate tables thought so and I guess we did too.

When we bid UCLA adieu we also said good-bye to the little rattletrap that had taken us back and forth from campus to the apartment we shared. The old German car was fine for impoverished students; now we knew we were ready for bigger and better things. Before long we bought a brand-new car. It was the first step of our upwardly mobile journey that eventually included bigger apartments, investments, and, at last, a home in the suburbs. Our lives were progressing the way they were supposed to, and we had the pretty new car to prove it.

After my husband filed for divorce, the car became the only tangible memento from our early married years that remained. By the time he moved out it was no longer pretty or dependable or enviable—it was tired and intolerant of past abuses. I didn't realize how closely I identified with the car until it died last month.

I'd assumed that the engine trouble was another of the quarterly aches that usually plagued the dear wheezing machine. Another car-repair bill, another few days in the shop, and my old friend would be home again to trundle the boys to the hockey rink, me to the grocery store, and the three of us to visit out-of-town friends. When I took my spluttering and shaking car in, I should have realized that it is unnatural for car-repair garages to greet customers with first-name familiarity. I shouldn't see a mechanic so often that he knows me and my sons the way the cleaners, pharmacy, and grocery-store people do. I should have known better.

The garage called the next day and in a Forest Lawn voice the mechanic told me that my loved one was as good as gone forever. They'd tried their best but it seemed hopeless. Of course I was welcome to get another opinion, schedule more lab tests, etc., but they felt that their diagnosis was dead on. I hope they realized that I didn't appreciate the pun.

So. Here I am without a car. I haven't bought a new one yet because I keep stalling for time. When the washer and dryer broke I cried, when the dishwasher stopped working I developed dishpan hands, and when the garbage disposal conked out I shrugged my shoulders. My life has been at the mercy of machines since I became a divorcée, but with the death of my car I admit that I feel truly victimized.

I was unaware of any feelings of real sorrow when my appliances broke—I was frustrated, maybe even angry, but I wasn't sad. This time, I feel a great sense of loss. I miss my old friend. Perhaps it's for the best—the part of my life that the once-enviable car represented had already died. It would only have been a reminder of times long passed. I've outgrown the suburban niche I once occupied and I guess I've outgrown the car as well. But, like any old friend, tangible or otherwise, who leaves the scene, it will be missed. Which, I guess, is the way it's supposed to be.

Now I have learned, thanks to my deceased auto, that I am as subject to hubris as the next woman. An event that occurred last week forced me to admit that I've spent a great deal of time the past few months patting myself on the back and congratulating myself on my ability to cope on my own in the big city. Ah, independence! Ah, resourcefulness! Ah, the joys of single womanhood! But what happened recently made me take another look at my self-image of invincibility. I was dismayed.

After my car died I discussed the matter over breakfast one morning with my ten-year-old son. We decided (1) that our family couldn't survive in Southern California without an auto and (2) that there wasn't much cash on hand to purchase the kind of car we wanted. So we agreed to think about our alternatives instead of rushing into a nearby dealership waving a checkbook and foaming at the mouth.

On my return from work that night my son and a man he evidently knew—he "knows" practically everyone in our suburb—were waiting for me. I was introduced to the fortyish friend, Mike, and patiently listened to my son's explanation that his friend owned a car dealership. He was going to help us "get any kind of car" we wanted.

Mike pulled out a little book and a sheet of Xeroxed questions. I was heady with the exhilaration that I was actually going to negotiate a deal on my own—the challenge! the excitement!

Mike smiled at me and our conversation went something like this:

"Now, what kind of car do you want?"

"Well, I'm not really sure," I answered.

"Well, what engine power do you need for your type of driving?"

"Uh, I guess just the regular kind."

"Do you care about two- or four-door?"

I shook my head. At this point, Mike grunted.

"Lady," he said, in a voice that reflected the fact that he was losing his patience, "what is important to you in a car?"

This question I could answer. I looked him straight in the eye, tried to look knowledgeable, and said, "Color. Color is very important to me, and I'm quite partial to yellow."

He looked heavenward. My son started to squirm. Mike asked, "Okay, how much do you want to spend?"

"Well, that depends. If I sell some more articles and if that book deal goes through I could go top of the line," I said confidently. "On the other hand, I won't know for several weeks if that will happen or not."

"Look," he said, obviously trying not to lose his temper. "Let's say that tomorrow your salary were cut in half. How much could you afford to spend if that happened?"

He was beginning to perspire and his face looked alarmingly red. I knew I had to be truthful, like the more ethical business people, so I said, "If my salary were cut in half tomorrow I'd starve."

"Well then, lady," Mike said, "you have no business buying a car." With that he shook my son's hand, said goodnight to me through clenched teeth, and left. Although he said nothing, I could feel my son's chagrin.

Mike taught me that, like it or not, I'm going to have to do some homework if I'm ever going to be a competent consumer. Buying a car is evidently far more complicated than picking a new dress or choosing a new piece of furniture, but I guess all facets of independence carry their own burdens. It was a chastening experience to realize that my son—two decades younger than me—knew more about EPA mileage estimates, cylinder compression, and rpm's than his mother.

After the bedtime story had been read I leaned over to give him a good-night kiss and he said, "You know, Mom, a silver car would probably look much nicer than a yellow one."

I tousled his hair, kissed him goodnight and, smiling to myself, decided that choosing a car might not really be that complicated after all.

22

Broken-Down Repair Shop Blues

I've learned in the past several months just how many things I can do without. I can survive without a husband, without a great deal of money, even without a car. The one thing I've got to have is a typewriter. That is a necessity.

Since I haven't owned one of those nimble machines for a while, I've been at the mercy of people or places that would let me borrow for a few hours the ways and means to type an article or two. Victor, a onetime coworker, learned of my plight and decided to let me use his old IBM electric typewriter that had been in storage for the past few years.

He brought the typewriter to my house when he arrived to join our family's annual tree-trimming party last December. The gathered friends greeted him (and the machine he brought) with undisguised warmth. Everyone knew that a typewriter was the best possible holiday present. Victor assured me that it was a good, hardworking machine and, though it might need some minor tune-up, it would be a worthy medium for my messages.

I woke up early the next morning, anxious to take the IBM to the repair shop and, with a little bit of luck, begin typing a new long-overdue column. I lugged the heavy typewriter to my borrowed car and drove the few miles to the local typewriter hospital. The man behind the counter said that the only thing wrong with the machine was the Selectric ball, which was obviously, he said, beyond repair. I accepted his diagnosis, he put a new ball on the spindle, and typed "Now is the time for all good men to come to the aid of their country." With a flourish, he ripped the paper out, smugly showed it to me, and said the bill was twenty-nine dollars. I gladly gave him a check and again hefted the heavy machine back to the car, returned home, and placed it on my desk.

Practically drooling with anticipation, I started to type. Everything went well for about three sentences. But when I typed an apostrophe I got an accent mark, as in día. When I typed a semicolon I got the Spanish tilde, the sign over the n in cañon. Other surprises like upside-down exclamation points greeted me every time I had to type something that was not a bona fide member of the English alphabet. Since it's not too easy to type a twelve-hundred-word column without the use of commas, periods, apostrophes, question marks, and semicolons, I realized that I was in a real predicament.

Once again, my eyes misty, I trudged back to the repair shop. In an even but imploring voice I explained why I had returned. With a show of embarrassed apology, the man put a new ball on the machine—an English one. This time he typed "Once upon a time there was a papa bear, a mama bear, and a baby bear." But before he could complete his favorite fairy tale he pressed the return key and moaned. With a forlorn face he explained that I would have to leave the machine at the shop. He said it needed a tune-up, a lubrication, and a new platen. I shrugged, longingly touched the machine's keys, and returned dejectedly home. After a suitable postoperative period, I returned to the shop, checkbook in hand, to retrieve the typewriter. I was all too aware of the backlog of articles at home and the increasing impatience of editors who had listened to my excuses about deadlines unmet. This time the man behind the counter told me that the bill was thirty-seven dollars. I gladly paid, caressed the typewriter, and spirited it away from the hated repair shop.

I decided to start my new project first thing in the morning. After hopping out of bed and making a fresh pot of coffee, I inserted paper and was appalled to see that this time there was no ball—Spanish or otherwise—on the machine. After a few curses and an extra large serving of coffee cake to calm my frazzled nerves, I was back at the repair shop. By now I was in a mood to kill.

I placed the typewriter on the counter and waited for someone to assist me. The three men in the shop had seen entirely too much of me in the past several weeks and instinctively knew I had not dropped by to pay a social visit. They cast lots and the loser approached the counter. We started at each other like the gunfighters in *High Noon*—needless to say, I played the righteous-anger role immortalized by the late Gary Cooper. Before the repairman could speak, I outdrew him.

"Would you like to guess what's wrong this time?" I asked. "We don't play games here, lady," he said, "you tell me what the problem is." Choking with rage and frustration I said, "It won't type." I could feel tears welling in my eyes.

He was forced to agree with me and reached for a ball, avoiding my eyes. Soon he was typing, "It was the best of times, it was the worst of times, it was the age of wisdom, it was the age of foolishness . . ." But before he got to the part about light and darkness, hope and despair, he turned the machine off.

Sheepishly he said, "I just can't let you take the machine home." The déjà-vu experience interfered with my ability to absorb his words about balance and backspacing. I only remember his embarrassed request to call him on Monday.

I left the shop in state of shock. Could it be that no one had worked on the machine during its previous internment? Could it be that each time those people fixed one part they broke another? Could it be that they had extra-high heating expenses last month and my repair bills were their only way to meet their financial obligations? Could it be that they know I'm a single woman and no one is going to come in and, using Baretta-like friendly persuasion, force them to quit disappointing me?

As much as I hate multiple-choice quizzes, this time I'm going to have to answer "all of the above." But my answer will not—at least for quite sometime—be typed. I'm still on pencils and pens.

23

Leaving on a Jet Plane

I'm hopelessly behind schedule. If all goes as it should, in only forty-eight hours my son and I will be in a hotel room in the Big Apple, not home in our Southern California suburb. It'll be my third trip east in as many years. It'll be my ten-year-old's first, but we are equally excited and nervous—I because I know what to expect; he because he doesn't.

My bedroom floor is flooded with suitcases, tissue paper, and clothes that seemed perfectly suited for Manhattan when I wore them in the department-store dressing room. Now that they're in the honest light of my room I can see that they're totally, totally wrong. At the rate I'm going, our suitcases will never get packed. And, too late, I find that all my lists and plans and preparedness have been for naught.

The contact-lens cleaner is ready. So is my son's wardrobe, my newspaper columns, my book manuscripts, my hopes and fears; everything I could possibly need in New York is safely tucked away. It's time, I've been told again and again and again, to get my traveling word-and-writer pony show on the road. My mentors have urged me to go to New York, to set up my stories and my thoughts and let the powers that be take a good hard look.

Now, too late, I find I am afraid. I'm afraid the people in Manhattan will not read, or worse, that they will read and laugh or scorn or ignore. I am afraid of being artistically on my own, without buffers or intermediaries or protectors. I keep looking for a sign that the guardian angel I used to believe in is still on the scene, waiting to be stuffed in a suitcase next to the nighties and the hair rollers.

In the hubbub of packing and planning we've not forgotten our ritual Monday night "Little House on the Prairie" viewing; work on a term paper; an art assignment about nature and life; the oohing and aahing over long-overdue school photos; one bath; one shower; two new versions of "Here Comes Peter Cottontail" courtesy of today's kindergarten class; a display of shock and alarm (by me) at my elder son's apparent inability to spell or punctuate the way my imagined natural-born Rhodes scholar should; a long talk about hurt feelings; mutual tears; and, finally, a three-way round of warm good-night kisses.

I return to the tissue paper and the plane tickets convinced that only single mothers have trouble coordinating the lives of their loved ones. Everyone else, I'm positive, lives more smoothly along the uncluttered path of fulfillment—only my life, I silently whimper, is so unfairly sabotaged by school assignments, spelling flaws, and unstylish clothes.

I can only hope that last-minute arrangements and necessities will take my mind off my troubles and keep me occupied until my brain can be reprogrammed, preferably to be productive.

After all items are gathered and all piles are packed in

the right places I reward myself with a pacifying cup of coffee. Now that the house is quiet and everyone else is asleep, I can admit that the sense of well-being I usually feel before a trip is no longer with me. Tonight, when I need it most, it has apparently gone on strike. Suddenly the thought of flying to a city of powerful strangers, in the hopes of enticing them to pay me (handsomely, I hope) for what I'd gladly do for free, leaves me homesick before I even leave the house.

I do feel very frightened. I want to take along an emotional bodyguard—the bald book-review editor with his mischievous blue eyes and encouraging smile; or my surrogate big brother who has made it *big* as a writer and expects—demands—nothing less from me; or the girl friend who quietly listens to my hysterical tales of deadlines and galleys and heartbreaking disappointments, but continues to believe in me when I doubt myself.

I desperately want these people to be with me and hold my hand and help me through the difficult birth of a dream come true. Already I can sense that I'm going to need all the help I can get to survive these particular labor pains—and I need to turn to my friends for a bit of mental first aid. It's a futile cry. I know all too well that no one can make this journey more pleasant for me. It's my chosen game. Whether I win or lose, there'll be no one to whom I can pass the buck.

So tomorrow my son and I will board the plane and mentally wave good-bye to safe, warm, friendly L.A. I will see the freeway montage and the Pacific and the Ultrasuede mountains recede from view as the 747 carries me to a meeting I've waited and planned for my entire life.

Four years ago on "The Waltons," John-Boy, the would-be writer, went from West Virginia to New York in hopes of selling his manuscript. He had written the book, lost it in the fire that destroyed his family's home, and had laboriously restructured it. When he arrived at the editor's office he encountered a busy, overworked woman whose vision was obscured by the stacks of unread manuscripts ominously surrounding her desk. John-Boy, clutching his work, was unsophisticated and sincere enough to beg the editor to read it (and like it). She did (and she did). John-Boy was then able to embark on a life that allowed him to be forever grateful to New York for making his dream come true.

I've remembered that TV episode—it stayed with me when I only wrote in my journal, and when I was too depressed to write at all, and even when I was writing so much that my entire existence was dominated by paper and pencils and pens. Now the story is going to be not only John-Boy's, but my story too. I'm going to pound the pavement and sit waiting in reception rooms and I'm going to hope against hope that New York will be good to me and that I can forever be grateful to her.

I secure the locks on the door, turn off the lights, check on the sleeping boys, and tiptoe across the obstacle-course floor to my bed. I crawl between the covers and try to will myself to a good night's sleep. Behind schedule or not, I know that my clothes and my child and my columns are going to be on that plane tomorrow. I'll be on it, too, and so will my dream.

24

New York! New York!

E. B. White once wrote that New York ". . . can destroy an individual, or it can fulfill him, depending a good deal on luck. No one should come to New York unless he is willing to be lucky."

When my son and I left for New York I was more than willing—I was ready, waiting, and eager. And terrified. I felt that the honchos who live in the Big Apple would either welcome me with open arms or slam doors in my face—and bunkhouse logic or no, a little voice told me that I was taking a big risk.

My friend who had advised me to travel alone and leave my son at home was—blessedly—wrong. My son fell in love with Manhattan (just as I had years before) the moment he stepped off the plane. Months and months of being the man around the house could not be altered simply by a change of locale. He grabbed luggage and hailed taxis as proficiently as any New Yorker and I decided that I could at last thank TV for apparently teaching him a useful thing or two.

He began making friends as soon as we arrived at our

hotel. I'd often wondered if I'd know so many neighbors if I lived without kids; the trip to New York forced me to admit that they were my prime social conduits. From the doorman to the bellhops to the waitresses in the coffee shop, my son immediately made first-name basis friends. By the end of the first day I felt as if I were living a real-life *Eloise at the Plaza* existence with a ten-year-old who knew far more about a big-city hotel than I would ever learn.

As soon as we began to make our rounds—me with my manuscripts and him with his Judy Blume book—I realized that I had the perfect arrangement. As we visited agents, I paid close attention to the boy's reactions, which I knew to be uncannily on target. Before I could comment on my judgment of the person we'd met, my son would give me a pint-sized personality profile. From "He's really nice" to "She wasn't very friendly" to "I like the way she runs her business," his opinions were invariably incisive.

After a long day of pounding the pavement, my son asked if I'd really meant it when, back home, I'd promised I'd take him ice skating in Rockefeller Plaza. I assured him I'd meant it. He said, "Then I think we should go now, Mom. We need a break." And while a big part of me wanted to fall on the bed and kick off my shoes, another part of me wanted to forget about credits and bylines and fees and editors and agents. So I took off my New York suit and changed into my California jeans and left the briefcase and the book behind. We skated and drank hot chocolate and ogled the outdoor scene until we agreed that this was surely New York at its finest.

One day we rode the subway—a terrifying prospect until we met an eighty-year-old lady who entertained us with subway stories and stayed with us until she had seen to it that we'd safely reached our destination. We journeyed to the financial district for lunch with my *Wall Street Journal* editor; we shopped for kids' clothes and Beverly Cleary books; and we began to feel right at home in the middle of Manhattan.

There were, in my week-long stay, only two appointments to which I could not take my son. And though I worried about leaving him alone in our room I soon realized that I needn't have. By the time I returned—sore of feet and soaring of spirits—my son had socialized with the doorman, the elevator operator, and the garage superintendent. Chattering simultaneously, I told him of my warm reception at *Vogue* magazine and he told me about the money he'd earned helping the doorman handle the taxi overload. Obviously, this called for a celebration! So, just like Eloise, we did what all young-at-heart-hotelers do: we ordered fancy desserts from room service.

During our stay we shared meals from Chinese to Scandinavian to Greenwich Village Italian, and made ourselves equally at home in the Rainbow Room and the World Trade Center. We discussed the outlook for my next year's earnings, the possibilities of getting a book contract signed before we returned home, and each day's tally of new writing assignments. We missed our friends and sometimes felt lonely for home, but we agreed that the entire experience was heavenly.

When I'd completed my rounds with newspaper, magazine, and book people, we started to pack for the return trip. Crunched amid the F. A. O. Schwarz goodies and the Lord & Taylor bags, we found an overflow of bundled-up memories that pulled us home on the one hand and begged us to stay on the other. Like a gambler who is finally winning, I knew I had to leave New York before too much greed set in.

On the flight home, I was too jittery to read or chat or

even give silent thanks for the nicest week I'd ever had. So I did what I always do when immobilized—I wrote. I wrote a travel piece, a book review, a column for the newspaper, and had the plane not approached Los Angeles airport so quickly, I would have been tempted to start the Great American Novel.

When I was finally back home, I stumbled around in a glow of good luck. I'd received the assignments I'd longed for, I'd interviewed the people I'd been asked to write about, and I'd found a publisher who would not only talk to authors, but was nice to them as well. I'd given my son a glimpse of the people who populated his mother's world, and I'd seen New York through a child's eyes. And since we were both more than willing to be lucky, New York managed to give us only the best. Reason enough to always be grateful to the Big Apple—and to E. B. White.

25

---◦⊃∞⊂◦---

My One-Year
Anniversary

In my family, there has always been a big to-do over the passage of time. My parents, who were well into middle age by the time I came along, felt that the innate foolishness of youth could be eliminated if only the young would realize how short our allotted life-spans are. They may have been right.

During my childhood, the brevity and wonder of life were forever dramatized during the annual events that celebrate the passage of yet another year. Birthdays were special. Thanksgiving, Easter, and Christmas were sacrosanct. Anniversaries of all sorts were to be remembered according to custom.

December 31st was a day earmarked for lists of achievements and changes realized during the past 365 days; my father would painstakingly quiz me, from the time I could first grasp the concept of time, on how I planned to change and improve during the coming year. So you see, time, in our family, was quite obviously regarded as a tool for improvement and for the conquest of the impediments that life might scatter in our path.

The ever-changing power of time was reflected by my parents' belief that time could alter the unalterable. Flights of overexuberant confidence or a childhood grand mal would invariably be met by my father's favorite maxim that "this too will pass." As I've grown into adulthood, the pattern of annual checklists has stayed with me. Almost reflexively, I chart my sons' growth—physical and mental—in terms of "only a year ago." The annual marking of events and traditions stays with me, if for no other reason than to serve as a reminder that I am not nearly as avant garde and free of childhood habits as I might like to think.

A glance at the calendar the other day reminded me that one year ago I officially joined the ranks of the divorced. My husband's departure catapulted me into a new phase of life that nothing from my earlier life had led me to expect. When I was a girl, the security of marrying your high-school sweetheart was considered a guarantee of doe-eyed compatibility forever. Never, during the years when I considered myself happily married, did it occur to me that "this too will pass."

My ledger sheet of the past year on my own has taught me some valuable lessons. I have learned, first and foremost, that rebuilding one's sense of dignity and worth is no easy job. When I became a divorcée my long-deceased parents were not around to remind me of the transitional nature of my sorrow or fear. The sense of aloneness—which Gail Sheehy tells us in *Passages* is the crux of the human condition—is terrifying to a woman when she loses her husband to the so-called charms of another.

I've learned my mistake: relying for my security and sense of value on a man and his feelings toward me. I now know those good feelings must begin with me and then spread to those with whom I share my life. I like to think that, if nothing else, my once-backward thinking on this topic has been reversed during the past year.

The past twelve months have also been a unique opportunity to learn about the value of friendship. During my decade or so of marriage, I'd formed alliances with people I considered to be friends merely because they attended my parties, ate my food, and drank my liquor. My husband's business cronies (or women in the PTA) became automatically accepted as friends because my life never demanded that people with whom I socialized be anything more than "jolly good fellows." When my economic, social, and marital status was turned upside down, I learned far better ways to judge the merits of relationships. I learned that the few people who could listen or advise or lend a helping hand were far better "friends" than those who used a husband's values as a Rorschach test for their own marital concerns.

I learned that my children—maybe all children—are far more resilient than I might have believed. The boys who were confused and embarrassed by their father's departure learned that parents are not infallible nor is life predictable. They learned at a very tender age that parental decisions are sometimes made for reasons that children cannot comprehend. My sons no longer ask "when" or "if" their father is coming home. They know we are now a family of three and they have grown accustomed to the hectic pace that a one-parent family demands. They are no longer threatened or frightened by divorce—they count themselves among the millions of school-age survivors of adult discord. I have learned that my children are light-years ahead of their mother in reliance and strength and independence. I have learned to be proud of their ability to adapt.

I have learned how to deal with finances—how to pay bills and save payment stubs and do the many money-related chores that were an unexpected (and unwelcomed) "benefit" of being on my own. One year ago, because I had a live-in banker who knew money the way I know metaphors, I hadn't the faintest idea how to tackle taxes or make installment payments or ask for credit—now I do. Perhaps the biggest benefit of my first year as a divorcée has been learning that even though I went from my father's to my husband's home, I really can cope with life without a man to clear the way.

Had my husband never left, I might never have had the chance to learn how to deal with broken ten-speed-bike gears or damaged hockey helmets or cracked windowpanes. The intricacies of reporting a theft or asking for a job or patiently explaining long-division homework assignments would have been cheerfully, if foolishly, relinquished to the man of the house.

It's true that the loneliness and the fear and wonder of being "mateless" (when everyone else in the world seemed to have a partner) were expected penalties of an unexpected divorce. But the serendipitous side benefits of learning how to cope by myself were—and are—a happy surprise.

I no longer rue being left for another woman and my sons no longer feel abandoned or rejected. Whatever losses we endured have been replaced by newer enthusiasms, fresh commitments, and an underlying layer of self-reliance. We've been forced to go along without him, and it hasn't been nearly as calamitous as we once feared. A year ago I wish I'd remembered daddy's maxim that "this too will pass." Now I know at firsthand that he was right, so right.

26

My Make-Believe Family

When I was married, I gladly adopted my husband's family. My father died a few months after our wedding and I was left with an aging mother and a couple of far-away cousins. I accepted the challenge, after years as an only child, of entering a ready-made family, which included a new set of parents, a sister, three brothers, and a husband. After years of living in a quiet, subdued, small family, it was exciting finally to be a member of a "clan."

Ever since we met in 1965, these people have played at center stage in my life. I watched a sister go from a young girl into a mature woman and I saw little boys—younger then than my younger son is now—develop into a full-grown men. I was there for birthdays and holidays and graduations, and since I had so little family of my own I seriously worked at chronicling and gathering and nurturing my adopted family-by-marriage. I was the one who traced the family tree and took the family photos and gave the family parties. They knew me as well as—or possibly better than—they knew the man I married. And I got to know them pretty well, too.

I learned the difference between a real family and a make-believe family when my husband said good-bye. For a self-proclaimed devoutly Catholic clan the dilemma of divorce should have been traumatic. It wasn't. My husband received from his family, his first Christmas away from the boys and me, more appliances than we'd been given as wedding gifts. And his mother's proud donation of a coffee pot—"so he wouldn't have to drink any more instant"—was the most clear-cut endorsement of his departure I could have imagined. It was not what I had been prepared to see. Divorce brings lots of surprises.

After he moved out, I soon realized that in his family's eyes I had lost my once seemingly secure niche. Probably because they didn't want to interfere, there were no phone calls or cards or invitations from his brothers. Family picnics and parties and holidays were attended by his new girl friend, not his old wife. They'd seen her often enough at my house so she'd never been a stranger. Now she was more than a friend.

"How," I wondered, "can they do this? Can more than a decade of feelings be replaced so easily?"

I should have realized that the answer was yes. What was important was not whether "he" had done the right or the wrong thing—or even whether he had done it gently or harshly. What was important was to present a solid front—a family front—to drown any nagging fears or suspicions or embarrassments. Hopelessly outnumbered, I surrendered. Having grown up an only child, I was unprepared for the "united we stand" front that a big family usually presents. An occasional call from his sister would be my only indication that someone—anyone—felt sad that I was no longer their brother's wife.

This family-front issue came up again recently when one of his brothers wrote me a letter. I had not heard from this brother in almost a year, so the letter was a surprise. What it said was even more of a surprise. After three pages devoted to descriptions of his home, his job, and his new locale, he finally asked how I was. And then he said, "I know feelings are strained between my family and you, and I'm truly sorry for that. I hope and pray for the day when pain is healed and troubled relations are better. I do not spend my time speaking poorly of anyone, and I hope the same can be said of you."

The veiled admonishment seemed odd. That paragraph taught me why his family could never really be my family—adopted or otherwise. My family—small as it was—believed that if you chose to act a certain way you had to swallow the lumps of public opinion that accompany those acts. In other words, you had every right to act as you wanted but you had no right to expect people to cover up or to clean up your deeds. In fact, the knowledge that people would not be quiet about your peccadilloes was oftentimes enough to force you to scrutinize what you were contemplating to make sure it was what you really wanted to do.

I now see that my ex's family expect—demand—silence. It's not enough that their son behaved with less than gentlemanly sensitivity. Now we must all pretend that he did not do what he did. This benign silence is so very different from my family's habit, when attacked, to stand up and say, "Of course I did it. And I'd do it again if need be."

It was hard to see his family forget about my loneliness during the holidays as they went to have dinner at my husband's girl-friend's home. It was hard to see them ignore my lack of family, my broken heart, or my sense of fear and bewilderment when he left. It was even harder to see them smilingly welcome the presence of my friend, my replacement, in their newly reorganized family circle.

It's still hard, even now, to understand their picture of what really happened in hopes of a nicer, more palatable version for the neighbors. Now that their children all live far away, now that they want some visitors, and now that their son and his new wife are out of the country, they may realize better what life is like without a family.

My friends have told me I'm a fool to continue to include them at my children's birthday parties. "Where were those people when you and the boys needed them?" they ask. Fool or not I still send invitations for every birthday and I wonder what they think as they actually see my boys growing up in a fatherless family. I shake my head at how complicated my reconstituted families have become.

27

I'm Not a Writer,
I'm an Actress

You probably think of me as a writer. That's fine, because I see myself that way, too. I've just learned I was wrong. That I spend my days pinioned to a typewriter is inconsequential. What I really am, you see, is an actress. Really.

I made this startling discovery more than a month ago, cast in a role that other divorced mothers have probably rehearsed for decades. None of my girl friends had choreographed their part quite the way mine had been, so I was somewhat unprepared for the demands made upon me. Now that it's over I can write about it. I could even graciously accept a Tony, Emmy, or Oscar if anyone felt impelled to hand one out, but I'm not going to hold my breath. Divorced moms rarely get awards. I'd like to think we get better things, even though the Screen Actors' Guild and the Academy of Motion Picture Arts and Sciences might disagree.

The way I discovered my hidden, untapped reservoir of dramatic talent was, like most surprises of my recent life, at the hands of my ex. In spite of some legal magic and a fair-minded judge, I realized that my sons were going to have to be away from me to spend some time with their father during the Christmas holidays. They've visited with him before—but not at his new faraway, foreign home. Before he went abroad, my sons simply went up the street to the house where both families had spent countless hours together—before, you'll remember, my friend became his wife. She and I used to have the same type of dishes, funny stories, children, and hockey in common. I'm still not used to our also sharing the same last name.

At any rate, my ex lived in her home only a few months. Soon he was sent out of the States and now my sons were going to have to leave me, our neighborhood, and the country for a week with their "other" family. Situations like this call for cool thinking, efficient planning, and the ability to bite the bullet—talents I didn't think I'd muster under the circumstances.

A letter arrived containing round-trip airline tickets for the boys, out-of-country travel documents, instructions about what time to be at the airport, and a list of clothes to pack (God forbid that I should forget to send the Lacoste shirts! What would the country club say?) .

The departure day dwelt in the back of my mind all during the holidays as we baked Christmas cookies together, decorated the tree with our friends, and stood in line for the compulsory yuletide photo with the department-store Santa. I couldn't forget that my boys were with me now, but in *x* days—or hours—they'd be so far away that even to hear their voices would cost a cool ten dollars for three minutes. For a mother who is used to talking with her children hours each day, it was a mental adjustment I wasn't sure I could handle. I felt as if I were sending them not several thousand miles away, but into outer space. I'd never been to the city they would visit, and I knew nothing about where they would stay, what they would eat, or how they would live. Impossible!

Naturally I had to keep these and other thoughts to myself. It would have been easy—but most cruel—to let my sons know how worried and sad and apprehensive I was. My long-ago cheerleading experience came in handy. I became another Emmy-aspiring Pollyanna, our family's Mary Tyler Moore-ish chairman of enthusiasm. Packing the hated suitcases, eating lunch before going to the airport, trying to describe what "fun" it was to sightsee in foreign countries, I remained smiling and cheerful. What a performance! My sons saw no tears. I don't think they saw any sign that I was dying to go on the plane with them. They didn't know that I ached to be a part of the new experience they were sharing.

One of the side benefits of divorce: single mothers are forced to accept separateness from their children much earlier than married parents. We have no choice but to accept that our children have perfectly natural alliances that may have the power to make us fearful or hurt or angry or distraught. Our children, like it or not, are made to love and need not only us.

After arriving at the airport, checking the documents, and wrestling with the luggage, we solemnly waited for permission to board. I walked with my sons to the plane, maybe holding their hands a little too tightly, and helped them find their seats. I checked their seat belts, made sure their plastic name tags were fastened securely, and shared good-bye kisses. I asked the stewardess to please be nice to them, to please understand that this was their first trip in an airplane. She nodded and continued down the aisle on her inspection tour. When there was nothing more for me to do, I walked down the ramp, a heavy knot in my throat, and waved to my munchkins through the cold, foggy L.A. night.

The doors finally shut, the plane taxied down the runway and disappeared somewhere in the sky en route to foreign lands and a noncustodial father.

Thinking hard, I walked back to the car. Sitting parked in the tinsel-decorated parking garage, I realized that for the first time since the plane tickets had arrived in the mail, I could stop acting. I drove home slowly, wishing that the Santa Clauses, reindeer, and twinkling lights of the L.A. basin would lift my spirits. They didn't. I entered the quiet, dark house. It was a sad place. There were no Leggos on the floor, no disco music blaring from the tape deck, no voices, no noise, no children. I made a pot of coffee and decided to think about my new acting career.

I could tell I'd been a smash. There wasn't a dry eye in the house.

28

---•◦∞◦•---

New Year's

I am sitting alone in my kitchen, newspaper and fresh coffee on the table before me. The windows reflect the sunny, chill weather we have every year on January 1, and, as usual, there isn't a cloud in the sky. The floor is strewn from one end of the house to the other (in spite of our slapdash efforts at orderliness the night before) with confetti and streamers and other residue of people who joined me for my annual New Year's party. The end-of-the-year gathering has become a tradition among my friends, and I have come to expect to feel especially good, especially happy, on the first day of each new year.

The normal number of postparty sleeping bodies are scattered throughout the house. I am the only person awake amid snoring sleepers. They're on the sofa bed in the den, in the guest room, snuggled in sleeping bags in the children's room. In a few hours there'll be a big, communal breakfast. Lots of bleary-eyed people will rehash, over coffee, the gaffes and antics of the night before. For right now, I have sole possession of the solitude of a quiet house, a sunny day, and a new year just beginning.

Part of my good feeling comes surely because so many people commented on how much more fun the annual party has become now that I'm single. They are right. When I was married, the party invariably consisted of three groups—the people to whom we owed social favors but didn't want to reciprocate with a whole evening's time; the people whom, for business reasons, my husband felt should be invited; and friends. Nowadays the *only* people who are invited are friends. It makes for a less profitable but far more enjoyable gathering.

A few miles away a parade is starting in Pasadena. The weather will, as it almost always does, cooperate to the fullest to remind the TV watchers back east that California is, almost always, the land of surfers and sunshine. Even though last night I danced too much, ate too little, and enjoyed too much wine, I feel better this morning than I have in months. The beginning of a new year, another chance to sort out my life's problems, can't help but appeal to someone as determinedly, doggedly optimistic as me. New Year's Eve, for me, is a chance to bid good riddance to a past year's worth of bad luck, poor judgment, and unfulfilled wishes. It allows me to wipe the slate clean and begin a new year with no impediments.

Surrounded by neatly stacked liquor bottles and mixers, I decide to do what I try to do every year on this morning—assemble my "resolutions." Full of commitment, unmindful that I never seem able to stick to my list for a full year, I nevertheless decide that:

This year I will finally train myself to forget about the hurts inflicted on me by others. People who intentionally (or accidentally) are rude or thoughtless or snide when I need their understanding or patience will no longer have the power to drive me to tears. I will try to learn how to swallow whatever hostility I still bear against *him* and his lack of sensitivity and try to remember that negative feelings are counterproductive. I'll try to rechannel my energy so to attract positive vibrations my way instead of pushing negative ones onto other lives. Harried as I am, the last thing I can afford is to waste time and energy on people who are not worth it.

I will also try to convince myself that I'm old enough to cope with life as an adult. This year I'll prove to myself that I can succeed on my own and can manage without a man at my side. I'll make it my goal to train myself to stop looking at every man's ring finger to gauge whether or not he is "available." I'll learn how to stop feeling blue because I don't have a date, because I don't have a boyfriend, because I don't have a husband.

I'll also try to remember to help other people in this world who also happen to be alone—because of death or divorce or ill chance. I promise, no matter how lovely and exciting and full my life may become, never to forget how it felt to be sad and frightened.

I will remember that by the time my children go to school, participate in sports and hobbies, and spend time with their "other" family, that there are precious few hours left for me to share with them. Therefore, this year I resolve to try to make each day with them unique and warm in some way. There are too few days together for me to allow them to be anything less than special. I'll remember that the best legacy I can give my boys is time; I will spend time alone with each child each day, even if it's only in the kitchen, in the garage, or in the car. I will refuse to let the demands of my hectic existence force me to be a stranger to my offspring or him to me.

I will finally stop the silly habit of "expecting" things to happen. No longer will I expect appliances to repair themselves, cars to function flawlessly, or bills to disappear by magic. I will finally accept that I am responsible for my life and, with a little effort, can probably make it function as well as anyone else's.

I will, this year, remember to celebrate the little joys of being a woman alone—the freedom, the privacy, the opportunity for growth. And I will try to ignore or conquer the discomforts, big or small.

I will remember to thank whoever watches over and protects divorcées for blessing me with the friends and the strength that helped me cope with my first year as a single mother. I will remember to be grateful for the on-again-off-again ability to believe in a brighter future, and for all things that made the past year not only a year to remember, but the best year of my life.

And then I will roll up my sleeves and cook breakfast for the dear people who have shared with me the end of an old year and the promising beginning of a new.

29

Chad and His Friend, Dick

Lest we think that women are the only victims of unpleasant divorces, this is going to be about a man I'll call Chad.

Chad is a thirty-five-year-old banker, who probably wishes that 1979 could be wiped off the slate of time. Until January of that year, he thought he had a nice home, a happy family, a loving wife, and adorable twin daughters. He also thought he had a car and a good friend I'll call Dick. Dick and Chad both used to ride in my car pool so we saw each other for a minimum of an hour or so each day. A few years ago Dick quit his job—and our car pool— but Chad is still a member of our daily Glendale-to-L.A. commute.

Two years ago Dick and his wife and Chad and his wife attended a party at my home. They were a foursome that had obviously spent many happy hours together. Plenty of inside jokes and subtle wisecracks passed among the group. Chad wanted to stay until the party was over; the other three, particularly Dick, wanted to leave. They explained they didn't like to dance and really didn't know too many people. That was the last time I saw the four of them together.

The families had made it a tradition to spend New Year's Eve night together, and this year they followed their established habit. They spent the time at Disneyland so that the little girls could have as much fun during the day as the adults had during the night. It was the last time anyone will ever see the adults together as a foursome—Dick and Chad's wife announced shortly thereafter that they love each other and will be getting married as soon as their respective divorces are final.

Chad has been in a slump since January. He lost twenty pounds, stumbled around in a fog called "what did I do wrong?" for a few months, and received his legal baptism by fire in his first court proceedings. Dealing with problems like a wife who will let him talk to his girls on the phone only once a week (while she listens on the extension) ; continual battles over visitation rights; being forced to leave a remodeled house that he worked on every weekend for a year; losing his car because it was a gift from *her* parents so she retains sole title; and relinquishing 80 percent of his salary to pay for the house, alimony, and child support have left him black and blue and broke. After pleading for a reconciliation and trying to work out a way to keep the family together, Chad has finally decided that if she wants to leave him for another man, fine—but she's not going to take away his daughters. Practically everyone who knows Chad feels that he would be the better custodial parent. Everyone, that is, except his wife.

Most women who love their children are prepared to fight to the death for their offspring, and some fathers have used this innate protectiveness as a bargaining tool. I know; it was used against me.

The scenario goes something like this. The woman is

subjected to a Chinese water torture of continual demands and phony charges. After an avalanche of unrelenting threats like "You'd better be out of this house next month" or "I'm not going to make one more house payment" or "Don't think you're going to get the car," etc., the beleaguered wife responds with a version of "You can have the house, the car, the money—just give me my children." The husband graciously relents and then whistles all the way to the bank unless, that is, the wife has a very good attorney.

At least half the custody threats fathers file result in the reduced financial state of the mothers—but it doesn't really matter; the woman has what she really needs, her children.

In Chad's case something else is at work. Chad loves his girls, would make a terrific full-time father, and couldn't care less about the house, the car, and the money. Chad is the one who wants custody—but he's going to have a next-to-impossible time getting it. His daughters want to stay with their father, he wants them, but his wife refuses even to discuss the matter. Until the court forced her to relent, she wouldn't even let him know where they were for weeks at a time, much less see them. Those girls have become her only—and most effective—bargaining tool. She knows Chad will do anything rather than risk incurring her wrath and losing his visitation privileges. He's over the proverbial barrel; she knows it.

One night as I gave Chad a ride home from work—remember, he has no car—he broke down and sobbed. In a choking voice he said he just wanted to see his girls, read them a bedtime story, play with them in the park, take them to the zoo. Tears streamed down his face as he told me that he hadn't been able to be with them for several weeks, when he wanted with all his heart to be with them every day. I'd never seen a man cry like this before. I'd never seen such male sorrow, male hopelessness.

Those of us who know and work with Chad are praying that the judge who hears his case will investigate before making a knee-jerk decision in favor of the female. Not all mothers are created alike. Sometimes the parent best suited for full-time parenting is a man. For now, we agree that Chad's wife seems to be in a poker game and holding all the chips: the money, the house, the car, the new romance, and most important, the girls. And Chad knows the odds are against him in this game—a game with stakes far too high.

While we were waiting to hear the latest from Chad's attorney, an incident happened that struck me and my friends—as bizarre. I received a phone call—from Dick—that was alarming in its naiveté and presumption.

Since I hadn't seen or heard from Dick since the night of my party, I was surprised to hear his voice.

Dick immediately began to tell me about his divorce, about his new fiancée, about his business. The problem, you see, was the undeniably messy divorce. It seemed that Dick was getting hounded on all sides. He had to worry about his wife and her attorney, Chad and his attorney, his fiancée and her attorney. Dick also had to contend with his own problems and with his attorney. It was, he assured me, driving him up a wall. He was obviously hoping for some sympathy.

The purpose of his call, other than relating his many woes, was to ask me why everyone couldn't be friends in a divorce. You and I know that only a madman would ask such a silly question but Dick was sincerely perplexed.

"You remember," he said, "that I considered Chad to be a true and dear friend." I silently nodded into the phone.

"But now he won't even speak to me. When she and I get married I want us to be able to resume our friendship, but everyone seems to fight. My wife fights with my fiancée, my fiancée fights with her husband, and epithets like 'adulterer' and 'slut' and 'liar' are hurled back and forth over the phone. I think we should be able to drop all that and start to be friends again."

I listened to his tale of the latest hair-raising battle over child custody and visitation. Then he said, "Since you've been divorced, I just have one question to ask. Will I ever be able to be friends with my old pal Chad? Can I invite him in for a beer when he stops by the house to pick up the kids? Can we still go to football games together and stay up and play poker on Friday nights? Will the divorce craziness pass over the four of us and let life resume the way it was before I fell in love with his wife?"

I knew it was going to be tough to give Dick an honest answer. The picture of Chad holding photos of the twins was clear in my mind; how much this man missed his homelife and his daughters!

I remembered the hurt and the shame Chad had felt at seeing his wife and his friend together for the first time. I wondered why Dick even wanted to be friends—if he had his new sweetie (and had won her at the price of losing his wife's and Chad's trust), what did he need with Chad's friendship? A salve for a guilty conscience? And if Dick was so anxious to be friends, why didn't he try to dissuade Chad's wife from hiding the girls? I found it pretty difficult to believe that Dick cared about Chad or his feelings.

In the movie *An Unmarried Woman* the departed husband—so in love with a new woman he met at Bloomingdale's—can't understand the hurt, the anger, the fury his wife displays. He has what he wants but he needs the icing on his personal cake: his wife's blessing for the new romance.

I'm amused by lovers who want the whole world to love them just because they love each other. It's amazing that they can expect the people whose lives have been disrupted by a less-than-righteous romance to forgive and forget (preferably overnight). If the ousted spouses are angry, they have every right to be. They also, it seems to me, have every right to be disappointed, hurt, and even resentful. They're entitled (temporarily) to wallow in every non-productive emotion known to man. Time and the demands of day-to-day living will squeeze those feelings aside soon enough. Anger is a perfectly reasonable reaction to the loss of a mate. There's no reason to deny the already battered rejectee the small comfort of his or her short-lived cathartic feelings. It's amazing that after stripping a person of his family, his spouse, and his trust, Dick now wanted also to strip Chad of the right to be angry.

I cleared my throat and answered Dick's question. "No. Your life will never be the way it was before you fell in love with his wife. It's too hard to be friends with someone you feel you can't trust."

Then Dick hung up.

30

⸺⸱⸱⟨∞⟩⸱⸱⸺

Histories

I was immersed in a history book the other day, and my thoughts retraced my early years. The relics of the childhood I unearthed left me dismayed at the disparity between my first decade and my elder son's.

I grew up—as did most of my peers—in a haven known as America in the fifties. As an adopted only child of older parents, my life was quiet, dependable, and, if not austere, certainly far from glamorous. It was only unusual because my father was in charge of setting up territorial offices for his firm, so every two or three years our family pulled up roots, moved to a new town, and there life continued as it had before. My childhood was an amalgam of discipline-oriented private schools and riding, dance, and music lessons, as well as the constant presence of two exacting and solicitous parents.

With all the attention and pressure, I grew up as a precocious, adult-oriented child. My time was strictly parceled to meet each parent's expectations (sewing classes to satisfy mama, memorizing the Cabinet members' names to appease daddy). Even the time allotted to me was subdivided to allow x hours for my pony, y for reading, and z

for hobbies. My life was too full to allow boredom, and it was carefully choreographed by my parents to teach the lessons that they felt were indispensable.

My older son is ten. He is (would any mother say otherwise?) full of immense charm and boundless grace. He is attractive and polite and one of the few people in this world I can count on. He is not only my son, he is my friend.

But he is not being raised by two doting grandparent-like adults, as I was. He is being raised by a divorced mother. A single parent who must still—two decades later—divide her life into small compartments. These days the subdivisions are not centered on self-improvement chores; now they are limited to the daily demands of survival in the big city. The hours include two sons, running a home, writing assignments, a job, and keeping my sanity—in that order.

My son does not attend a different "lesson" each afternoon as I did. Skills that I had gained within my first ten years are not a part of the game plan for my son. There is no money for those extras and there is no one willing or able to chauffeur and sit and wait as my mother did for me.

When I was twenty-three and still studying ballet, I remember my mother's presence in a particularly difficult class. She knew I'd worked hard on serial fouettés and she gladly came to watch and wish me well. How different this is from the evenings when my son has sports practices! He's dropped off. I rush away to shop for groceries or run errands, then pick him up and we hurry home for a quick dinner, homework, and bed.

The quiet times I shared with my parents as a child—walks around the stables, sodas after practice sessions, or daydreams about the possible careers that might evolve from my lessons—have been replaced in my son's life by less expensive settings and less leisurely time schedules.

Since I imagined, when my sons were babies, that they would enjoy better opportunities than I had, my inability to make those daydreams materialize has been a bitter pill.

I wonder if I am shortchanging my son. When my spirits are low, I admit it hurts to know that he cannot depend on me the way I could depend on my parents to have the money, time, energy, and interest to guide me safely to adulthood. My interest is all he can be assured of. I know too well that these are the years when my son should be playing piano after school, or dancing at cotillion lessons, or taking a mare over a three-foot jump. And I ache with the realization that each day away from those disciplines could make life harder for him, so often I wish I could give it to him now. Not next year—*now*—when learning is as easy as breathing.

I fear that someday soon I'll wake up to find that he will no longer want—much less need—to know the things I know or grow up as I did. It will be too late soon, but I feel powerless against the passage of time.

There must be millions of divorced mothers right now who wish they could give their children braces or ballet or music lessons, who wish they could give their children the predictability and security their own lives had. But we can't—we can't even find it for our own lives, much less offer it to our offspring. When husbands and money and time fade away, all we can do is search and dig and struggle to find the gifts—the free gifts—we can give our children and ourselves. The advantages that come without price tags or time schedules are the ones we can give our children—and I hope with all my heart that they will cherish them as much as their mothers hold dear the faded, out-of-date memories of hours at the barre, piano recitals, and horse shows.

31

---•◦∞◦•---

My "Most Admired Women" List

The annual "Most Admired Women" list was recently published, giving me much food for thought. The national list includes names like Betty Ford, Rosalynn Carter, Barbara Walters, Jackie O, Anita Bryant, and others. All, I'm sure, worthy of their much envied place on the Gallup Poll's list.

Now, even though no one has asked, I would like to offer my own sampling of most admired women. It won't be national; you won't recognize the names. But if you're like me, you will probably have more in common with these women than with those on the national list.

I admire Helen Kerr, who married the same man twice. The first time Helen was nineteen (and stayed married to him for eighteen years); the second time she was forty-four (and stayed married six years). Believing his continual promises of improved fidelity and increased family devotion, she felt that she owed it to her daughters, to herself, and to him to try and give it another chance. Unfortunately, both times Helen was punished for her determination to see the good and shun the bad.

In spite of her husband's departures, Helen raised two daughters, worked as hard as she could to give them a home, an education—and a sense of humor. Today she admits she is older and wiser but she hasn't lost her seemingly innate ability to laugh at life and at herself. Working with Helen on a day-to-day basis has taught me the virtue of being able to believe in a better tomorrow and in the value of smiling when there's nothing to smile about. I admire her kind of spirit.

I admire Vicki, a tall, beautiful blonde who made the mistake of marrying young and dropping out of school to work her husband through college. Vicki wound up alone after he received his diploma—another victim of the old "never put your husband through school if you want him to remain your husband" adage.

Thinking that you could earn a man's devotion by helping him earn a degree is a mistake Vicki and I both made. I met Vicki soon after her divorce when she came to our office to work; we've been friends now for close to a decade. After several years of the same office grind, she realized she was going nowhere fast. It was pretty obvious that there would be no hopes of promotion until she had a college degree of her own. It was also obvious that no one was standing in line to help her earn it. Rather than struggle with night school and a B.A. earned at a snail's pace, Vicki quit her job, drastically reduced her standard of living, and enrolled as a full-time undergraduate at UCLA.

Finally, last year, thanks to hard work, determination, a shoestring budget, and the encouragement of her family and friends, Vicki graduated with honors. Vicki is now a vice-president with a prestigious international cosmetics firm. Vicki could have spent years berating her not-so-chivalrous husband and hounding him for cash. She could have gone through life getting whatever she could get on the basis of her spectacular good looks. She could, as so many of us do, have done whatever would have taken the least amount of effort. But Vicki chose to work, chose to learn (rather than lament) from her divorce, and chose to get what she needed on her own. Vicki did it the hard way, but she did it—and I admire that.

I also admire Joyce Camp. Joyce is a pretty woman who, although almost thirty, could easily pass for nineteen. She is lively and cheerful and has a nonstop sense of humor. Joyce works as a manicurist in a small beauty shop in Burbank. Her days are spent listening, filing, listening, buffing, listening, polishing, and listening. The women who traipse in and out of the shop probably think Joyce doesn't have a care in the world—but she does. She is a widow with a seven-year-old son.

Joyce's young husband died of pneumonia six years ago, leaving Joyce enough insurance money to pay for the funeral expenses. He also left a baby who probably wouldn't remember his daddy. Joyce had never held a job and had no money in the bank. After the funeral, she realized she'd have to leave her baby and go job hunting even though she had no real work skills and no desire to be anything other than a lifetime stay-at-home mommy. With plenty of bills, a lot of sadness, and a baby dependent on her, Joyce faced less than pleasant prospects in the job market.

Joyce is not maudlin or terminally depressed—she is cheerful and efficient and determined to give her son a good start in life. Manicurists don't earn gargantuan salaries, but for Joyce the pay envelope at the end of the week represents a beginning. She had to work as a supermarket checker and save money to take the training for her job and she is rightfully proud of her new ability to earn a steady, if not substantial, salary.

Sometimes Joyce is sad: when she misses her family in

Iowa or when her son wants the things that other children have—things that are beyond Joyce's budget. But she is determined to give him a safe and happy home and to teach him that love and optimism have no price tags. And I admire her for that.

Los Angeles is full of women like Helen and Vicki and Joyce, women who have been disappointed but have somehow managed to swallow their hurt and believe in a better tomorrow. I can't help but see nobility in these everyday women—something that affirms for me the concept that productive hard work is good, and immobilizing self-pity is bad. Self-reliance and optimism is the only way of life for the thousands of women who wake up to find themselves husbandless and hungry in the big city.

When I need a large dose of sisterly inspiration, I call to mind these women. Unknown to pollsters, to news services, or to the public, they're the type of "Most Admired Women" that appeals to me best.

32

The Willison Way to Wealth, Fame, and Happiness

It takes remarkable presumption for me to write about the path to success. But people-watching has become a serious pastime of mine, and invariably gives me much food for thought—which eventually turns up in these pages.

Women whose marriages have failed are faced with frightening dilemmas. Most of the more immediate problems revolve around money. So now we will have a word about money.

I hope you were more familiar with the words that will dominate your postdivorce existence than I was. They're nice words. So I've been told. If you know them well they can, it is rumored, become dear friends. In my case, it hasn't happened yet, but always the optimist, I'm sure someday I'll strike up more than a speaking acquaintance, if not a close friendship, with the little guys called debits, credits, interest, and balance. I'm even going to try to get to like the old "you owe us" grouch.

Since I was married to a banker, it seemed logical that my familiarity with literature and French would be useless amid the household complexities of depreciation, income averaging, points above prime, and other foreign phrases. I couldn't have been more mistaken.

When my husband moved out I soon realized that in addition to coping with the devastating problems of emotional and romantic withdrawal, concerns about children who were bewildered by the chronic absence of daddy at the dinner table, and deep feelings of personal *Angst,* I also had to learn about—shudder—money.

The largest role I had played in the drama of our family finances was signing papers—legal and financial—whenever my husband told me my signature was needed. Like most women, I trusted the man I loved and wrote my name beside every little checkmark on scads of papers. Most of the papers I signed were fine; a few—like the one refinancing the house right before he moved out—weren't. The amazing thing was that I was financially ignorant by choice. I'd taken several accounting courses at UCLA, but cultural conditioning or, more likely, laziness convinced me that someone else would worry about money. Someone else like my husband. He was a banker and, after all, that's what bankers are for, n'est-ce pas? It was fine for me to limit my worries to my writing, the children's birthday parties, and entertaining my husband's business clients. Or at least I thought it was.

All of this may sound vaguely familiar to you. Few of my friends—married or otherwise—really know what their bank balance is, how much they owe, what their net worth is, how much they must pay in fixed overhead each month, etc. I understand why women would rather concentrate on more "interesting" subjects—I understand it well. But, like everyone else, I now have 20-20 hindsight. I now see how silly it was for me to have willingly remained so oblivious to the importance of money. Women raising children on their own can't pooh-pooh dollar signs. No one else is going to pay the bills or earn the money or provide for the small people in your life.

Your maternal visions—like mine—might have been ethereal images of kissing sleepy-eyed children good-night while tucking them into bed, or laughing together while skating at the ice-skating rink, or sharing popcorn on a cold winter night. Holding an infant in your arms, you probably never envisioned that school shoes, or doctor's visits, or bicycles would be a huge part—your part—of raising children. Even if you're lucky enough to receive regular child support, you still must juggle that money so as to make the best purchases for the children's physical, emotional, and educational needs. And you need to be well prepared to distinguish the "musts" from the "might-be-nices."

At the center of the money issue for single mothers is work—as in employment. I'll be the first to say that sewing pajamas, making cakes, or pruning the roses is work—but who is going to pay you for doing those things? Few divorcées have the economic wherewithal to stay home, to continue living on the same scale as they did when married, or, even worse, to go back to school to get sufficient training to support themselves adequately.

If ever there is a perfect Catch-22, it happens when you accept the fact that you must go back to work. Divorcées must usually forget the jargon about meaningful careers; what they must get is a job. The grocery bill, rent, and car payment can't wait until you get your degree or pass the bar. The bills won't wait—the schooling will have to.

Sounds bleak? I prefer to see it as a wonderful and exciting challenge finally to do what you were really meant to do. Had my husband agreed to help me get some post-graduate training, I probably wouldn't be doing what I most love to do—writing. The fact that he had someone else to spend his money on turned out to be a blessing in disguise. At the time, of course, I was hurt and disappointed—after all, I'd worked so he could get his master's degree; all I wanted was for him to return the favor. Now I see how lucky I was that he chose to spend his dollars elsewhere—it may have been the luckiest thing that ever happened to me.

Because I was stuck with low-level office skills and a degree in literature and French—like a thousand other females in Los Angeles—the job market didn't exactly pursue me. No one seemed to recognize my potential, my needs, my ambition; people were only interested in my typing speed. A dead end if ever there was one. But a dead end that bought school shoes, paid the doctor bills, and kept the car running.

Judith Rossner, author of *Looking for Mr. Goodbar* and *Attachments,* is largely responsible for my lack of bitterness toward dead-end jobs for females. She wrote several years ago about her life as a divorcée and her efforts to see to it that her writing be recognized and (financially) rewarded. One of the keys to her later success was her monotonous job. Rossner rose at 5 A.M., wrote till seven, woke her children, fed them, took them to school, and then went to her boring file-clerk job.

Each day held the same pattern—but while she was doing moronic slave-wage work for someone else, she was thinking—thinking for herself. The next morning those thoughts went on paper. Eventually those thoughts were on the best-seller lists and Rossner was on Easy Street. She claims that if she had had an exciting, demanding job there would have been nothing left over for the work that really mattered to her—the work Rossner, if no one else, knew she was meant to do.

I like Rossner's story. I identify with it to an uncanny degree. But the important message I'd like to convey is that each person must—better sooner than later—decide what she likes to do. What you enjoy doing is probably what you do best—and what, in the long run, makes you happy. Whether other people appreciate it or not—or are willing to pay for it—is not so consequential. What's important is that it makes you happy. Now, if you have to be a waitress or a typist or a bus driver to pay the bills, that's okay. But keep plugging away at your dream—it could be music, or writing, or acting, or caring for children, or working with pets. Whatever it is, do it.

While you're squeezing a few hours of pleasure each week out of your "calling," very important things will be happening: (1) you'll be doing what you want to do, (2) you'll be sharpening your skills at whatever it is, and (3) you'll be building a reputation. Someday, someone will remember that Mary Jones is a terrific pianist or that Sally Smith has the most remarkable watercolor technique, and when you're ready to break loose you'll already have established yourself in other people's eyes—as well as your own—as an artist, a singer, or a writer.

Some people might label me a Pollyanna for believing that dreams can come true. But with my kind of dream there is little risk—the bills still get paid while you do what you have to do to be true to yourself. You may not get rich and famous, but you will get something equally important. You will get the satisfaction of knowing that you have a talent, of whatever nature, and have used it to the best of your ability regardless of what other people thought. Many rich and powerful people in this world got that way by doing things they really didn't want to do.

I, for one, would rather do what I feel I'm suited for—and take my chances at achieving fame and wealth. If you're lucky, like Judith Rossner, you can sometimes manage to get it all.

Now you know why I get impatient when I see women grimly worrying about law school and M.B.A.'s and doctorates when they realize that their husband's paycheck has taken a powder. I'd like to see a lot less time spent on earning degrees and a lot more time devoted to learning enough about yourself to know which path to follow. Deciding which way to go is far harder than completing whatever journey you choose.

Being happy and successful and employed need not be mutually exclusive conditions for divorced women. Remember that a few short years ago Judith Rossner was also a frightened divorcée struggling to pay the bills. Rossner's story reminds me that a dream can come true—as long as you're willing to work at it.

33

Learning How to Be a Man in a Household That Has No Man

Ever since my ex moved away, my sons see him only on rare occasions, which are busy, activity-filled visits. While my ten-year-old may long for quiet, private times alone with his father—a slow walk, just the two of them, to the park and an afternoon spent shredding leaves under a tree and talking—he has cheerfully reconciled himself to the fact that this dream is close to an impossibility. He has adjusted, instead, to large gatherings, family reunions, crowded football games, and trips to the toy store.

All this is good—certainly better than what many broken-home boys get. When I hear stories about children who never spend time with their parents I'm grateful that my children are friendly—if not intimate—with their father.

But last night a neighbor asked me about the problems I'd encountered due to my son's lack of exposure to men. I was disturbed when she pointed out how few hours my son spent each year with his father. She wondered how he was "turning out." Now I wonder if something important isn't missing from the lives of my boys. I wonder where my son is learning—or even *if* he's learning—how to be a man. I'm painfully aware that I can teach him academics, cooking, budgeting, entertaining, worshiping, and—God, I hope he learns this—laughing. But how in the world does a mother teach a son how to be a man?

A part of me desperately hopes that it is something that doesn't have to be taught. As his blond hair and blue eyes just magically appeared, so, I hope, will the masculine traits evolve that he'll need to help him through life. He is acutely aware, even at his young age, that he is the "man" of the house. Without being asked, he assumes parts of the role he saw his father play: he locks the doors each night, takes out the garbage, shuts off unnecessary electric lights in the house, and brings flowers for my birthday and Mother's Day. I'm not sure if this is a good or bad sign—I just know it happens.

Will my son—since I don't have a father, an uncle, a brother, a husband, or even (alas) a beau to take him fishing or throw a football or build model cars—learn to be a man when he only has a part-time father? Perhaps, like so many such children, he'll learn from teachers, TV, books, peers and neighbors which traits are worth emulating and which aren't.

I cannot imagine evolving into the person I am without the strong, if conflicting, contributions of my parents; my middle-aged mother and father each tried to outdo the other in teaching me what they each felt I would need to know as an adult. I can no more imagine what my life would have been like with only one of them than I can speak Swahili. I feel it would have brought me a far less exciting adulthood. My father's determination that I androgynously learn to fish, change a tire, tar a roof, or trim the roses was, thank heavens, softened by my mother's insistence that I learn how to bake, knit, arrange flowers, and walk with a book balanced on my head.

Had my mother not been around I would have probably emerged as a Rosie the Riveter or a Josephine the Plumber; without my father's effort to dilute my Southern-belle mother's idea of a lady's role I might well have aspired to be a Scarlett or Melanie—helpless and frail and feminine and totally out of step with the times.

What about my son? As I write this he's dirty and reveling in the garage with grease under his fingernails, attempting to fix, for the fortieth time, a gear on his ancient ten-speed bike. It dawns on me, slowly at first, that he never saw his father's perpetually pristine fingernails dirty. He never saw his father take something apart and put it back together again. Where did he pick up this desire and talent to assemble and reassemble bikes? Not from his father and certainly not from me.

There must be a realm of role pattern and stimuli that is beyond the control of parents—single or otherwise. Perhaps my son will grow up to be what he is destined to be, regardless of my input or his father's or the TV's. Perhaps children carry a dream within them that is their own creation and for which we can neither take the blame nor the credit. We, as parents, can only try to make them comfortable with what they have chosen—whether their choice, by our standards, is good, bad, or indifferent.

One of the things that divorce and single parenthood has taught me is frequently and un-self-consciously to admit "I don't know." So I admit I cannot answer the neighbor who wants to know who is my masculine son's role model. I don't even know if he needs one, much less if he has one. I think that he—like girls who live with their fathers and other boys who live with their mothers—will develop according to his own drummer, in his own pattern, in his own time. And perhaps, just maybe, he will be better for it.

34

Everyone's Invited to the
Party Except Me

It may have already happened to you. If not, prepare yourself. Sooner or later it will. "It" is the hurt of finding out that your friends are having a party. They have invited him. They've even invited her. But they haven't included you.

The first time this happened to me, I was numb with disbelief. My son returned home from school one day to tell me that his friend's parents down the street—people I saw at church each Sunday, people who honked and waved whenever they drove by my home—were giving a party. I knew everyone on the guest list: people whose children went to school with my children, who lived in my neighborhood. At the time my husband and I weren't yet divorced—I was in the limbo of wondering if he would regain his senses and realize how much the boys and I loved him, or if he would actually decide to file for divorce and marry her. It's odd, now, to think back on those days and realize that the neighbors knew what he would do long before I did. But then they knew he was in love with her long before I did. And now I wasn't on the guest list—but he and his girl friend were.

Somehow I had to find a way to console myself and lick the wounds of being unwanted. The last time I'd felt so disappointed was in high school when I found myself tagging along to help girl friends shop for formals to wear to the Letterman's Ball. They had dates, but I didn't. Learning that my husband had been invited to a party and I hadn't propelled me back into teenage awkwardness with amazing speed. The trauma of being left out was almost enough to bring on an untimely siege of post-adolescent acne. But just as I survived having no date for the dance, I also survived last year's big party that didn't include me.

At church I still see the people who hobnob with my ex and his wife (when they're in town) . I still honk and wave and smile when I see these people who populate my home ground. I also realize that I'm no longer a part of their world—through their choice, not mine.

The fact that I am alive and breathing and living (alone) in their neighborhood reminds them that the world is not made up of two-by-twos. There are lonely people in this world, and sometimes they live on the same block, on the same street, or in the same neighborhood. I remind those people that their marriage could dissolve just as mine did. Someday they just might wake up and find themselves sad, frightened, and all alone even if they thought they had a good marriage. Those people probably don't like to be reminded of that part of the sweepstakes of life. Intellectually they're aware that illness, death, delinquent children, and divorce exist in our society. Emotionally they don't want to accept it. It's far easier to accept a couple, who have each divorced their mates in order to be together, than it is to accept the people left behind. At least the new couple reinforces the old-fashioned belief that there's a someone for everyone. And we all like to have our beliefs reinforced.

I don't feel angry with those people. They hurt my feelings and let me down when I might have needed them; still I can't muster up anger. When new incidents hurt my feelings or friends do things that are thoughtless I review my litany of past kudos received. And for every disappointment, I have a good memory that cancels the hurt.

Because I was black and blue with apprehension after my divorce, I was probably too slow to believe in other people's capacity for altruism. After all, I reasoned, if the man I'd loved for over a decade could prove to be so disappointing, whom could I trust? Fortunately, with the passage of time, my cynicism has been diluted by the many kind acts of this world's big-hearted people.

I remember my girl friend, Donna Agins, who called me every morning and every evening (toll calls all) for six months to make sure I was okay, to see if I needed anything, to see if she could help me cope with my problems.

I remember my attorney, Bob Schibel, who never complained about my phone calls to his home, my hysterical renditions, my untimely habit of crying, my inability to pay, or my reliance upon him for guidance and friendship and strength.

I remember Gloria and Patrick, who heard that my refrigerator was broken and knew I had no money to buy another. They appeared on my doorstep one Sunday afternoon, refrigerator and all, and proceeded to install it amidst my questions and shock and delight. They did it without being asked, without being paid, and without expecting anything in return.

I remember Benjamin Stein, who took me to dinner to calm my nerves the day my marathon divorce proceedings were finally over. He offered time and money and love and anything else he and his wife could do to help me and my sons get back on our feet. And he assured me, when I was most in doubt, that everything would turn out fine.

I remember Alex Campbell, who replaced my water heater when my basement flooded, who dealt with the gas company when they'd disconnected my service because I couldn't pay, and who never mentioned a word about repayment or reimbursement for his time or his trouble.

I remember Toni and Bob Sherman, friends for over a decade, who insisted that I spend each Christmas holiday since my husband's departure with them. When I was most inclined to feel my own shortage of relatives, they stepped in to remind me that there is more than one kind of family a person can have.

I remember the people who went to the courthouse—people from my church, my neighborhood, my office—to help see me through the three most unpleasant days of my life.

I remember the kindness of people who had either been through a divorce and remembered how unpleasant it could be or who were sensitive enough to realize a human was suffering—for whatever reason—and needed help.

I remember the neighbors and the teachers and the coaches who gave my sons a "little extra" love and time and attention to try to help compensate for their father's departure. I remember.

And when I become depressed over the people who were not thoughtful or gentle or sensitive, people who felt I could no longer assist or entertain them, I try to call to mind the lessons I've learned from friends who do not turn away when you're down and think you're on your way out. A divorce teaches you, with alarming swiftness, exactly where you stand with every name in your address book, and I'm willing to bet that the ones who reach out when you have the least to offer are the ones capable of teaching you the most valuable lessons of all. At least that's how I remember it.

So when I'm not included on guest lists or when people make thoughtless comments on my single-mother-status, I try to think about the good things that have happened at the hands of my friends. Then I put myself in the other people's shoes and wonder if I would have done the same thoughtless things they've done. Maybe I would have felt that it was easiest to include the neighborhood sweet-hearts and exclude their left-behind spouses. Maybe I would merely have wanted to have an even number at the dining-room table. Or maybe I would have felt that the other women at the party would have more in common with a housewife who didn't work than with a divorcée who does.

Maybe, but I like to think not.

35

Divorce Cruelties

Not long ago, *New Woman* magazine featured an article about a woman who had married a man she deeply loved, discovered he was having an affair, survived their painful divorce, and went on to care for her two children and rebuild her life. Needless to say, I strongly identified with the story.

One aspect of the story in particular reinforced a theory I have about such tales. The constant element about sordid divorces is the baffling element of cruelty. I know it's there, I've seen it time and time again. I still can't understand why it exists.

I wish that when a partner decided to leave the marriage (due to the magnetic pull of an extramarital affection) the deed could be accomplished by (1) honestly announcing the presence of another person, (2) explaining that the marriage is over, (3) expressing some "Thanks for the memories," and (4) resolving to make the transition—emotional and financial—as easy as possible. That is what I'd like to see. Instead I've seen treachery heaped upon skulduggery topped with cruelty. A simple explanation for the misdeed I've witnessed would be to say that nastiness exorcises guilt, but I still don't see the necessity of adding insult to injury.

When I hear stories of third-party divorces, I'm shocked at the ensuing financial and custodial battles. I can't help but wonder—an exercise in futility, I'm sure—why the new sweetheart isn't enough to appease the departing party. It would seem to me that once you got your heart's desire, the last thing you'd want to do would be to battle over the remnants of a buried marriage.

A case in point is a man I know named Karl. He accidentally discovered that while he was working at the office his wife was having an affair with another man. Of course he was crushed. Not satisfied with knocking the wind out of Karl, the two lovers proceeded to parade their passionate affair in front of him, his friends, his coworkers, and anyone else who would pay attention to them. Sticking the knife in, you see, wasn't enough—they had twist it to validate some perverted notion that Karl was incapable of feeling and was, therefore, fair game.

And then there's Rachel. Rachel and her husband had been married for fifteen years when he told her about his new girl friend. Rachel and Sam had gone all through college together as sweethearts; they didn't have any children and seemed, to those of us who knew them, to have a remarkably close relationship. Sam fell in love with a lithe, blonde *shiksa,* young enough to be his daughter. In addition to diagramming point by point all of Rachel's imagined shortcomings, Sam took pains to remind her that, unlike his new girl friend, Rachel simply made him feel old—and he was now determined to stay young, preferably forever. Even after the divorce, Rachel could count on seeing Sam's teeny-bopper bride whenever he came by the house—he was almost compelled to remind Rachel that she was (as if it were something to be ashamed of) nearly forty, to remind her that he had picked out the youngest replacement he could find.

Matt also went through an unpleasant wrenching at the hands of his ex-wife. Matt is an elementary-school teacher, gentle and patient and best described as "mellow." Matt's wife was tired, after eight years, of her teaching job and the quiet life she and Matt shared in their suburban neighborhood. She told Matt she wanted a Mercedes, diamond earrings, a bigger home—she wanted, she said, to "live." She taunted him, as she prepared for their upcoming divorce, with reminders of his lack of money and her need for (and worthiness of) the finer things in life. And she made sure that he knew that she had left him for an affluent man in the jewelry business who would provide her with the things she so obviously "deserved." Is it any wonder that Matt felt less than a total success by the time his divorce was final?

The fact that men and women who fall in love while married need to leave such a bad taste in their spouse's mouths must have some sort of logical explanation. Maybe they want to make sure that their ex never tries to tempt them back. Maybe it's a final way of purging themselves of years of unspoken anger and disappointment; or maybe it's the animal instinct that mindlessly reacts to the smell of fear with increased aggression.

Whatever the reason, I've seen the same tasteless scenario in so many third-person divorces that I can't help feel sorry for the person who's leaving. They get their freedom and they frequently get their new playmate as well. But I tell myself that it's a Pyrrhic victory for all that, because they must also get a lot of things they didn't bargain for: postponed guilt, haunting regrets, and permanently rearranged self-images. The cost to them of rubbing salt in other people's wounds is exorbitant. What they have to sacrifice to get their farewell vengeance must surely be more valuable than anything lost in a measly property settlement. What they lose in order to mete out pointless emotional retribution is priceless, but then the cost of cruelty has always been pretty high. That's what I tell myself.

36

---◦◦◦---

The Weed in My Garden
That Won't Go Away

There are psychological terms for the malady I possess—
some call it neurosis, others say it's a preoccupation with
preparedness, others claim I have a procrastination phobia.
Whatever name you want to use, I accept the charge—I'm
a compulsive planner. I am stubbornly determined to
make things easier for me and my tomorrows. I like to do
my Christmas shopping in July. I try to buy my boys'
clothes ahead of time so they can grow into them. I buy
toothbrushes by the dozen so I don't have to worry about
running out, ad nauseam.

Each spring I get to bury myself in my favorite plan-
ahead activity—flower shopping. My sons and I have a
ritual every year when the bulb catalogue arrives from
Holland showing page after page of multicolored flowers:
hyacinths, daffodils, jonquils, crocuses, irises, anemones,
and, of course, tulips. I'm as enchanted by the names—
Duke of Windsor, Merry Widow, St. Brigid, Blue Aegean,
Burgundy Lace—as I am by the flowers themselves. Unlike
my mother, I cannot name flowers at sight, nor can I
immediately identify one strain of rose from another. The

extent of my horticultural skill lies in picking the pictures that most appeal to me, writing the check, mailing in the order form, and—the part at which I excel—waiting. My sons and I wait months for the bulbs to arrive and, after they are safely planted, we wait months for the flowers to appear.

Springtime at our house is a protracted surprise party. Whoever finds the first crocus or daffodil leads the rest of the family outdoors to share in the excitement and delight of a serendipitous discovery.

I'm devoted to pretty springtime flowers because of two lessons they teach. First, my garden is the most obvious way tangibly to teach my children that you really do reap what you sow. Since actions speak louder than words, the bulb-planting ritual at our house should eventually—I hope, I hope, I hope—demonstrate to them, along with other demonstrations, that ill will and selfishness and stinginess will come back to haunt them as surely as generosity and forgiveness and kindness. Next, the idea of postponing gratification is best learned in the garden, and I hope my young ones can carry the lesson of the power of time beyond their own property into the big bad world. That's at least what I hope our springtime flowers can do for them.

What my garden and its flowers do for me is entirely different. Their purpose in my life is a little secret, of which my children are totally unaware. As any divorced mother knows, there is precious little security in our day-to-day life. The foreclosure notices and the unpaid gas bills and the continual threat of growing inflation and shrinking child-support checks make for a life that's best planned on day-to-day survival. Like Scarlett O'Hara, we must push worries and problems and disappointments to the back of our minds and resolve to think about them "tomorrow." But my family ritual of planting bulbs defies the probabilities of disaster because the act of investing in a yard—a garden—on property that might possibly not be ours by the time the flowers bloom is a small but positive way of thumbing our noses at adversity. In weak moments, each daffodil that blooms reminds me to dig my heels in and fight whatever woes lie on the horizon. As I look at the tulips and irises I'm reminded that when we planted those bulbs last fall we had plenty of problems. But here it is—spring! The problems have been either endured or replaced. Those flowers are the most immediate possible reminder that time is on my side.

A flower garden is a small thing to most people, but to me it's more than a haven for butterflies and bumblebees. My flower garden is a small sign of my commitment to my family's home and to our future together, even if I can't remember all the flowers' names.

In my horticultural worship, an unsettling event took place yesterday that practically ruined my entire day. It had been a beautiful spring day. Before breakfast my sons and I had oohed and aahed at the daffodils and narcissus that had—finally—blossomed. My lesson to them of reaping what you sow was being reinforced by the visual reward for our planting labors the previous fall. Even the dwarf peach trees were sprouting blossoms and, on that first balmy day of the year, it seemed as if the rainy season—and winter—had finally come to a close. My faith in spring and in the ultimate outcome of good was restored. By the end of the very same day my optimism and sense of the sublime would be sorely bruised and shaken.

After a day of deadlines at the office, I returned home to the customary sight of my five-year-old waiting for me on the porch step. As usual, he came to greet me as I got out of the car and we walked to the door amid chatter of his latest kindergarten triumph. He explained that his big brother was at Little League practice and continued about the exciting things that had happened during his day.

While he prepared to show me his daily crop of school papers I glanced at the mail—an ominous-looking letter was waiting, courtesy of my ex. I opened the envelope and read his latest. It was on his vice-president's business stationery and was full of "re's" and "i.e.'s" and "cc's." I was not impressed.

The purpose of his letter was to let me know that for the first time he would take the boys for the summer vacation. He told me—not asked, not suggested, not offered—that he would have them for six weeks beginning July 15 and continuing through August 26. Period. A week at Christmas had been hard; this was going to be impossible.

Tears welled in my eyes before I even reached the second page of my orders from headquarters. I folded the letter, made a mental note to call my ever-helpful attorney first thing the next morning, and reviewed the crayon-colored papers my little one had brought. I reminded myself to see to it that he gets a haircut soon, and gave him a quick hug as he left to play with a friend across the street. I was left alone with the hum of the refrigerator, a hot cup of coffee, and a deep feeling of dread delivered via airmail.

It would be marvelous if, like, say, Katharine Hepburn or Rose Kennedy or Lillian Carter, I could summon words of wisdom and comfort from some inner reservoir to allay my fears. But I am either too sad or too young or too frightened to be stoically rational. I am numb.

I wonder what it will be like for my boys to be far, far away from their friends, their neighborhood, their lifestyle, their mother for six weeks. Will the allure of country-club living make our all-too-suburban life seem all too dull when they return? Will they reacquaint themselves with the comforts of having a daddy at the head of the table (and a stepmother at the foot) and be dissatisfied with the single-parent life they now accept without question? An endless stream of questions rushes through my mind.

After dinner, after homework, and after the merits of a new baseball mitt are discussed, I try to read in the house, now finally quiet. The steady sound of children breathing emerges from the bunk beds they share, and I envy the peace of mind they now enjoy.

Safe in my own bed, I toss and turn and try to sleep. Pointless. The arrival of the letter has forced me to admit that a mother's vulnerability never ends. There was a time when I felt that a judge's final decree would end the trauma of a disenchanted husband. Then I felt that his immediate remarriage would free me because it would keep him too busy to annoy me any longer. After that I hoped that his transfer to a foreign country would forever end my pain. Now I sit in bed while the rest of the city sleeps and ask myself if I'll ever, *ever,* be in a position where his wants and needs and musts don't infringe on my own.

My flower garden, tonight, just doesn't have what it takes to calm my frazzled nerves. But tomorrow, maybe tomorrow it will.

37

---·«⟨∞⟩»·---

Sex and the Single Mother, or Romance on the Rebound

People complain that I never write about sex. They're right, I never write about sex. Lest you think I'm in some way abnormal, I'll admit that I am not uncomfortable having sex, but I am uncomfortable writing about it. To soothe the imaginations of readers who wonder just how boring my private life is, suffice it that I have gradually begun to date regularly; my children have never caught me in a compromising position; I have never lived with a man who was not my husband; and I am not a virgin.

Since I don't want to betray my innermost feelings about the worth of the multiple orgasm, I will deal with a subject I am not uncomfortable writing about. Romance. It's the precursor of sex for most women old enough to remember a Cary Grant/Audrey Hepburn Saturday-matinee movie. If you're too young to have gone to the movies on Saturday afternoons, turn to the next chapter, please.

What I'd like to talk about is the bygone allure of dating.

Romance is a subject near to my heart because it allows two people to display their more fanciful sides first. And whimsy is hard to resist. So this is first for women who want to hear what I have to say about dating: then I'll tell men what I wish they knew about women who've been in love and are not afraid of falling in love (on a date) again.

You might as well face it—sooner or later you, as a single woman, are going to be faced with your first date. After your husband has left, after you've weathered the storm of single survivorship, you will finally open your eyes and decide to enjoy life—or try to—again.

Until you make that decision, the issue of men or romance or flirtation or sex will be moot. But something happens to women (and men too) when at last they turn their back on the unpleasantness that has happened to them. Some invisible signal goes up to the opposite sex and the dating game begins. Only it's very different now than before you were married.

When my husband left, I was a twenty-seven-year-old mother of two who had spent her twenties as a wife and a mother. I found singles bars and encounter groups as foreign as the Dalai Lama. Two of my divorced girl friends are currently planning weddings to men they each met in—yup—bars. This prompts a "You did it! You did it! They said you couldn't do it but you did, you did!" salute from me—a mixture of incredulity, wonder, and envy. I, at least, know myself well enough to accept that bars—like the fraternity mixers of college days—give me symptoms akin to lockjaw, nervous hives, and terminal claustrophobia. It's a milieu in which I am miserably out of place.

For many, a drink after work presents an opportunity to meet someone new, to become reacquainted with the by-now-forgotten appeal of aftershave, and to learn the verbal give and take of the singles market. But if you are like me, feel free to avoid bars and/or one-night stands like the plague when looking for the companionship of a man.

What about the common habit of being "fixed up" by well-meaning friends? For me, this method, although not perfect, is certainly preferable to "stranger in the night" encounters in bars. At least when you've been fixed up you have some common ground—your relationship with a mutual friend. If your friends really care for your welfare and know you well, they will usually be able to screen out the prospects who would not appeal to you (or find you appealing). While these introductions can be awkward or embarrassing or disappointing, they can also be full of delightful and charming surprises. When friends have said, "We're inviting someone to the party we think you'll like," more often than not they've been right.

The last (and best) part of the dating game comes when you meet someone neither through friends, nor through your neighbors, nor even thanks to your children. It comes when that certain someone goes out of his way to get to know you. When you get the feeling—after all you've been through—that someone can still find you charming or pretty or sexy, it reactivates feelings that may have been dormant for years. That kind of magic can strike at the grocery store, in a playground, even at a hockey game. The important thing to remember is that it can happen.

Do be prepared: Dating as an adult is a very different game from high school or college dating. As single adults—and most likely parents—you'll unconsciously find yourself stripping away the little (and probably useless) issues that seemed so important when you were younger. Now you will both want to get to the heart of the matter. What does he want out of life? How does he treat children (his and/or yours)? Could this person be a friend as well as a lover? Before you know it you may be discussing topics you might never have discussed with a man before—because before your divorce you probably didn't realize how important certain things (like money, sex, privacy, children) could be to you.

Now about a few things I wish men knew. Either women keep their romantic "I wishes" to themselves, or else men aren't savvy enough to pay attention when subtle hints are circulated. If I had a younger brother, I'd like him to know what I hear—and I'd like him to hear it from a friend, rather than be hit over the head by a two-by-four at the hands of an exasperated woman ready to call it quits. Sooooo, I've gathered a few "wishes" from my travels. Like them or not, this is what I wish men knew:

I wish men realized that florist shops are not limited to the needs of the ill, the deceased, and bridal parties. ERA or no, few things work magic like delivered—to her office—flowers. I can't remember anyone hoping to receive a gift of candy since my fourth-grade Valentine's party, but rarely does a week go by without some friend lusting for a lover's bouquet. The man who sends roses with a note "Have dinner with me at eight?" or "You looked beautiful last night" or "I'm proud of your promotion" is not automatically guaranteed to get what he wants—but he will get a reputation for knowing the right thing to say and the right way to say it.

I wish men would ask a woman's opinion only if they really want to hear it. Too often, so my girl friends tell me, it seems as if a scenario has been printed on the man's shirt cuff: (1) order drinks, (2) comment on his day, (3) ask about her day, (4) switch off attention until it's his turn to talk again. Although vanity usually deters a woman from admitting to her date that she knows he's not listening, it would be nice (for both parties) to be spared such embarrassment. Asking questions to "appear" interested is poor form. If you don't care, don't ask. It spares your feelings, her feelings, and lets you both get back to subjects that you may genuinely care about. Play acting is hard work; a date is supposed to be fun.

I wish men knew that lots of women wished they would dress up. A group of six women were talking over lunch the other day and all agreed that nothing is sexier than a man in a tuxedo. One woman said, "the only time I see men in tuxedos is when I watch the Academy Awards on TV." The women all nodded. Reminiscent rumblings were heard about the now-forgotten charms of French cuffs, pajamas, over-the-calf socks, Gucci loafers, and tweed blazers. And not one of these women was over thirty! Fine clothes, sans chest hair and chains, may be gone, but their charms are not forgotten!

I wish men knew that standing in line for two hours to see a movie in Westwood is not romantic. It may be fun or offbeat or even entertaining, but it leaves something to be desired as an example of savoir faire. The same goes for dates consisting of attendance at Rams, Dodgers, Angels, Kings, and Lakers games. Women today—fettered with the demands of a career and/or children—get a little homesick for an honest-to-God romantic evening. They are too few and therefore much cherished by contemporary women. Sorry, but that's the way it is.

I wish men knew that single mothers who date consider it heavenly to have a man pay for the baby-sitter. The *Wall Street Journal* recently categorized single mothers as the new American poor, and by springing for the baby-sitting fee a man shows he understands the woman's predicament, that he is not intimidated by a woman's motherhood status, and, best of all, that he's not stingy.

I wish someone would set the record straight about so-called patronizing or condescending male/female behavior. No woman I know objects to having her door opened, her chair pulled out, her cigarette lit, or her door opened for her. Many women find such allegedly archaic good manners a definite plus. Conversely, every woman I know rankles when a man refers to a female forty-five-year-old vice-president as a "girl," or when not-very-clever double-entendre jokes are made to try to break the social ice; or when a man verbally appraises another female's physical attributes. A man who at the dinner table makes an approving remark about another woman's figure can usually count on his companion's yawns, glares, or silent disappointment. Gentlemen: If something is going to be said about the gorgeous redhead at the next table, let your date say it. At least that way you don't come off as a man with an uncontrollable urge to ogle every pretty little thing that crosses your path. I guess when it comes to sexism, women take spoken messages to be much more accurate gravity readings than the "gentlemanly" manners so many of us grew up with.

I wish men would remember to mark Valentine's Day, *her* birthday, anniversaries, etc., on their calendars. Women tell me that the men in their lives wouldn't dream of forgetting the Trojans' football opener, the Bruins' first basketball game, or opening day at Dodger Stadium. Year after year these same men "forget" to take the time to pick up a valentine, an anniversary gift, or a birthday surprise. The standard male excuse, which runs something like—"I love her every day and she knows it, so I don't have to make a fuss over so-called special days"—just doesn't hold with most women. A man can score countless points by remembering that every woman needs a little romantic pick-me-up now and then. Whatever time it takes to mark your calendar will be returned tenfold—it's the easiest way in the world to be an instant hero.

Throw away any lingering images of your "dream" person. They will only hinder your discovery that good things come in all types and sizes. Ms. Perfect needn't be drop-dead gorgeous, needn't be a cosmopolite, needn't be the queen of the tennis court. It's important to find someone who can accept you for your good qualities, tolerate the bad ones, and feel you're the best thing that's happened in a long time. After a divorce, people often need to feel they can make someone happy merely by being alive, and that's exactly what can happen when the Right Person comes along.

Whether you meet in a classroom or a bar or a drugstore, it really doesn't matter. All that matters is that you find each other—and what could be more romantic than that?

38

Vicarious Achievements

The other day I had a mind-boggling conversation with my friend Ondine. She was telling me about the problems her friend Sally was having.

"It's awful," she said. "Poor Sally is losing so much weight. She has huge dark circles under her eyes, she can't sleep, she can't eat. It's as if she's a human bundle of raw nerve endings. I can't help feel sorry for her—I so hate to see her this jittery and nervous."

I, sheltered creature, immediately assumed that either Sally's husband, a top Hollywood producer, was having a scandalous affair or else had decided to divorce the poor woman. Just like Ondine, I was beginning to feel the first stirrings of pity for Sally. I could picture the scenario: Dear, sweet Sally, like half the women in Beverly Hills, would have signed a prenuptial agreement that would leave her penniless and alone after years of marriage. Not wanting to appear overly nosy, but already full of empathic condolence for Sally, I asked Ondine if she knew what had happened to cause such distress in her friend's life.

Imagine my surprise: Sally wasn't suffering from a problem in *her* life—she was suffering because her husband had a big, multi-million-dollar deal in the offing and was unsure how it would turn out. Sally didn't know what to do about this suspense; she had become emotionally immobilized by the hoopla. The international offers, the huge sums of money, and the press corps' attention were just too, too nerve-wracking.

As Ondine continued her story about poor Sally's plight I could feel my sympathy dry up and blow away. It wasn't the media hype that upset me—it was the exaggerated display of vicarious empathy. What in the world, I wondered, does Sally's terminal case of nervous exhaustion accomplish? Does she really think it helps her husband's deal? Or her husband? Or herself? What a waste, I thought, what a silly, stupid waste.

I'd been on my own, I guess, long enough to forget that women could still get so wound up over their husband's (or children's) lives. I was appalled at the idea of Sally— or any woman—investing such an alarming amount of personal energy when she had to know that it was a counterproductive attention-getting gesture.

I'll admit that only a few years ago, I was guilty of the same misplaced enthusiasm. Once I held my breath in anticipation of my husband's raises and promotions. Once I felt that the only way for me to get "ahead" in this world was to ride on his professional coattails. Once I believed that I not only had to mirror his indignation or hopes or ambitions; as a good and faithful wife, I had to magnify them. That was how I once interpreted my wifely role and I know that there were—and are—countless women who did and do likewise.

Today I can't imagine that anyone else's business deals would make me lie sleepless at night. My wheels can no longer spin powered by the fumes of transplanted energy. A similar way of life used to work for me, but I'm happy to say that it doesn't any more. I still get excited and happy and sad, depending on the turn of events in my life, my children's and friends' lives—but I certainly don't get so immobilized that I can't function or help them. Not any more.

The change is not because I'm a single woman and not because an invisible insulating shell protects me from the ups and downs of other people's lives. It's because I have a life of my own that requires a giant chunk of my daily energy allotment. It's also because I finally learned that achievement by proxy simply isn't possible. I cannot benefit from someone else's glory merely because I am an onlooker or because I'd like it to be my glory. I also cannot lessen another person's sorrow or anxiety by adapting that hurt to my life. I can applaud or encourage or cry and I can share, but I cannot steal.

Until I saw the effort, energy, time, and hope I'd invested in my husband's education and career go down the drain I felt much differently. I once believed—ashamed as I am now to admit it—that I could be excused for not exerting the effort to build solid achievements of my own as long as I was a cheerleader for the accomplishments of others. I couldn't have been more mistaken. And I feel that Sally, and her chosen path of empathy, is wrong, wrong, wrong. The cheers ring hollow when they're for someone else, not what you could (and should) have done yourself. But I believe that they ring true when they're in addition to what you have achieved. I believe that disciplining yourself to use the gifts you have—however meager they may appear to you—enhances, rather than diminishes, your ability to encourage and appreciate and applaud others. For some mysterious reason women seem to have had a hard time accepting that idea—I know I did.

I feel so strongly about the futility of identifying with other people's accomplishments, I'm sure, because of my mother's example. When she was distraught or distracted or depressed she refused to brood; instead, mama followed the same advice she'd given me when I would become upset: "Do something!" Mama would bake or sew or care for her roses. Her harmless activities didn't make the stock market rise or improve daddy's health or cinch the scholarship I wanted, but they didn't complicate the situation either.

Ondine finally ended her tale of Sally's plight and then said she'd have to get off the phone. "I've got to keep the line open," she said, "Sally might need to talk to me." I told Ondine I understood and went to wrestle with the temptation to brood about the mystery of vicarious achievements. I wondered if I was really the only woman around who felt you could toot the loudest for your loved ones when you had a horn of your own to blow.

39

Little League

My son's Little League season is about over. The season isn't really over but since my son leaves before the end for summer visitation with his father, *his* season is over. For at least this year I've sat in my last bleachers, chanted my last "go, Monterey, go," and had my last gossip with the other mothers. A year ago I would have never imagined I would say this, but now I can admit that I think I'm going to miss it. What I'll miss most is the opportunity to see men devote time and energy not only to their children but other people's children as well.

A few months ago I spent the day with one of my married girl friends. We left the kids at her house to watch a ball game on TV with her husband. Fortunately, he didn't seem to bat an eyelash at passing his Saturday surrounded with three of his own and two of mine, so my friend and I enjoyed a day of shopping, antiquing, and giggling. When we arrived home, late in the afternoon, her husband was on the lawn passing the football to each of the kids. I was caught by the scene because it's something I don't often get to watch.

I was practically speechless with gratitude that my friend's husband would give my sons an experience they might not otherwise enjoy. After I told him what a rare treat this was for my boys, he went out of his way to include them on fishing trips and other activities. He may never know just how much those occasional outings mean to me or how valuable they may prove to be for my sons.

Although my dislike for baseball is no secret, I get the same gushy feeling watching my older son's games. Even though he hasn't displayed an inordinate amount of talent on the diamond, it was still a treat to see him functioning in a totally male environment. Since his school is coeducational, his home life is dominated by his mother and his housekeeper, and his free hours find him in a home punctuated with the arrival and departure of girl friends and female neighbors and coworkers, it comes as no surprise to me that sport has represented, for my son, a sanctuary from women. The feminist in me first rebelled when I saw this tendency. Now I feel he's as entitled to his time away from women as I am to my time away from men. So Little League has become a truce to establish and nurture his male identity.

I'm grateful to Little League for letting me discard some prejudices. It was not, as I'd assumed, a waste of time to sit and watch children pursue a little white ball. I watched the boys develop a sense of teamwork and an ability to yield the limelight for the sake of their teammates, and to learn some valuable lessons about humility, generosity, and obedience that might have been next to impossible to convey in a verbal way. I watched men try to teach little boys how to be gracious losers and dignified winners and players who could try their hardest whether the game was tied or close to hopeless.

My son learned to admire and like his coach as a friend

as well as a teacher. And I like to think that the coach learned that not all little boys play ball with equal skill or have the same kind of home life. My son learned that a good baseball coach doesn't have to yell or threaten or frighten boys into performing, and he learned to enjoy and expect the physical signs his coach used to express his emotions—a pat on the rear, a hug, a tousle of the hair, or two hands placed firmly on the player's shoulders. The boys learned to interpret these signals as well as they learned to slide into base, bunt the ball, or catch a fly ball.

I learned that sometimes my mere presence could make a world of difference for my son. He didn't ask me for enthusiasm or understanding or a slavish addiction to the game he was playing; it seemed enough to have me sitting and watching, although he didn't appreciate it one bit when I sat in the opponents' bleachers simply to join a friend who was sitting there!

I'll pack my son's mitt when I assemble the clothes for his summer visitation, and I'll have his uniform cleaned and folded and packed safely away with his cleats and bat and the now-disused hockey equipment. He won't be needing his Little League equipment for quite some time, but he will need to remember the lessons he's learned. I hope he's learned that his normally vociferous mother can, at rare intervals, admit she's been wrong. I hope he's learned that every experience in life has a hidden lesson or two in addition to the obvious ones, and I hope he's learned that you don't have to have a daddy in the house to enjoy the good feeling you can get from a father figure.

40

Summer Custody Countdown

This came very close to being an almost perfect Saturday night, at least as I like to live it these days. I followed my ritual of allowing myself, unlike most nights, the indulgent luxury of a few hours in front of the TV. Sandwiched between dinner, roughhousing with the boys, and bedtime stories, I've watched reruns of "The Mary Tyler Moore Show" (will I ever outgrow my identification with Mary Richards?), "Upstairs, Downstairs" (will I ever outgrow my love for Hudson and Rose and Lady Marjorie, as real to me as my own family?), and "Second City Review" and "Saturday Night Live" (will I ever outgrow my addiction to collegiate humor?). Will I ever outgrow TV?

While Friday nights are usually quiet, hours devoted to books and letters and written ways to recuperate from the working week, Saturday nights are another thing, though not what you may expect. Even though my son's altar-boy duties dictate an early Sunday morning alarm clock awakening and although I squeeze a week's worth of errands and duties into one day, Saturday nighttime still finds my engines purring and my mood, unlike the night before, light and cheery. I usually have to force myself to give in to sleep on Saturday nights and I always ask myself how one mere day away from the office can so drastically affect my frame of mind.

This Saturday I combined my favorite pastime with my most dreaded chore. The good news is that I spent scads of money on clothes; the bad news is that it was in preparation for my sons' imminent departure to visit their father.

I so live in terror of the single mother's indictment, which all of my divorced girl friends have heard from time to time ("What do you do with all the child-support money?"), that I periodically put myself in debt to make sure there can be no doubt that every dime I receive—plus a great deal more—goes directly to help my boys. The $190 I get every two weeks, which barely covers groceries, is somehow expected also to house, clothe, entertain, and educate them. My divorced girl friends refer to it as "fathers' folly" to expect mothers to accomplish so much when given so little. At any rate, I bend over backward to avoid the confrontations my friends have had to face and I go way overboard when it comes to wardrobe.

So this Saturday I bought the clothes for my boys' upcoming visit to their father's faraway home. I keep hearing about the country club, the fancy neighborhood, and the household help; since I don't know which reports to believe and which ones to discount, I follow the shopping list that I imagine will meet their summertime needs.

Pulling the list from my purse, I storm through the boys' department, gathering sports shoes, new penny loafers, dress slacks, tennis outfits, bathing suits, underwear, socks, and pajamas. By the time I pause to take a breath I realize I've spent the money I earn for two weeks of work in just under an hour! Had I not been overcome by a wave of longing to be with the boys as they play tennis or swim or sightsee in their fabulous new clothes I might have been inspired to mortgage the house and just keep on buying. The salespeople, remembering the wad I spent at Christmas, smilingly bundle up the clothes, remind me that I shouldn't wait so long between shopping sprees, and then escort me to the elevator with good wishes to have a happy summer with my sons. I refrain from telling them that, for the first time ever, I won't be with my boys this summer.

As we drive back to Glendale, I'm soothed by the cathartic knowledge that my sons' wardrobes will certainly be as nice as their affluent stepbrothers' and that I have again postponed the inevitable hints that I spend the precious little child-support money not on my sons but on myself.

Once home, the boys leave to play with neighbors and I slowly transfer the clothes from shopping bags to the waiting suitcases. The usual joy of buying clothes is gone. I finally admit to myself as I start to cook dinner that today was the saddest shopping spree I've ever had.

In due course I manage to get one boy tucked in bed; the other is trying to have what is currently referred to as a "meaningful dialogue" with his mother. We have had an indoor picnic dinner—homemade soup and saltines served on a tray in the boys' room. Sitting on the floor, surrounded by their toys, they slurped their minestrone while I read aloud the fantastic adventures of Mowgli. My younger son, soon tucked in bed, fell asleep almost immediately, lulled into dreams by Rudyard Kipling's word pictures of life in the jungle. The other son carried the empty plates and bowls downstairs and wanted not to sleep, but to talk. So we talked.

He asked the question I've heard a million times the last month: "How long until we go?" And I answered "two weeks." He nodded, sitting on the kitchen sink dangling his slipper-shod feet back and forth as if they could communicate as aptly as words.

"Just tell me one good thing that's going to happen," he challenges. So while washing the dishes I try to weave a tale that I can only hope will help to convince him. "Lots of good things will happen. You'll get to spend some much-needed time with your father, and he may even teach you how to play tennis. You'll improve your foreign-language skills, do some exciting sightseeing, and you'll be able to spend lots of time at the country club and go swimming whenever you want. I really think," I say with mock enthusiasm, "that it'll be a terrific vacation for you and your brother." His sullen silence tells me he hasn't bought my sales pitch.

"I don't want to go, mom. This ruins my whole summer," he says, "and it ruins Paul's and Mike's and Bobby's as well. They may not even remember me when I get back— in six weeks they could all have new friends. I can't even go to camp or do any of the things my friends get to do."

"Well," I hedge, "the people who really like you will still like you whether you're gone six days or six weeks." But even as I say it I remember the preoccupation with popularity of my childhood and I know my son is not altogether wrong.

"And," he continues, more intent on telling me his gripes than on listening to my solutions, "it ruins your summer, too. I don't like the idea of leaving you here all alone by yourself." I laugh at his preadolescent paternalism, but when I turn to hug him I see the tears in his eyes. He knows all too well that I've grown so accustomed to having a household full of activity that the idea of quiet and solitude is not unreservedly welcome. I set down the dish towel and give my son a hug. "Listen. I love you and you love me," he nods and wipes at a tear that has succumbed to the power of gravity, "and in six weeks we're still going to love each other. Just because you're going away doesn't mean I can't keep you and your brother locked in my heart—and no one can stop us from writing letters or calling or thinking of each other. Sometimes people find that a little vacation makes them appreciate each other more—and I know your friends will be really looking forward to the day when you come back home. Just like I will."

My son fidgets with his pajama buttons and I know what he is thinking. He is playing the same trick that I play when I must leave a place I don't want to leave. It's called memorizing. I can feel his eyes watching me as I return the clean dishes to the cupboard. I know he is committing the sound of the birds and the crickets to memory. There is no doubt that he is trying to form an imprint of the fragrance from the lemon tree and the rose bushes. It will, I hope, help him call his home to mind when he is thousands of miles away.

I'm trying to commit a few things to memory, too. I'm trying to remember the bicuspid that has just begun to erupt—a tooth that will probably be firmly in place when he returns home. I'm trying to remember his exact height to see how much he grows while he's gone. I'm wondering if he will be more manly or if he will still want to talk to me unselfconsciously in the kitchen when he returns. I wonder just how much growth and change can occur in six weeks—in my sons and in myself. Will I learn things when I live alone? Will I develop new ways of dealing with my single status that the constant presence of children has made impossible?

Even though I'm the one they're leaving behind, I have a hunch that I'm going to be making a few journeys of my own during the next month and a half. And I think

I'm as reluctant as my son to face the inevitable lessons I'll learn. Already I've discovered that I'm much better at giving pep talks to other people than I am at giving them to myself.

I tell my son that it's time for bed, and we walk upstairs deep in our own thoughts. I kiss him good-night, wish him sweet dreams, and close the door on my two most precious possessions, my boys whom I must share for a six-week stretch each summer.

Long after midnight I find myself still thinking about my son's misgivings. When I can laugh no more as I sit in front of the TV set, I go to the calendar and cross out day number fourteen and, like a thousand other L.A. moms, I make plans for countdown day thirteen. This Saturday night I do what I usually do on Friday nights to lift my spirits: I go upstairs and surround myself with books and paper and pens. Unlike my children, they at least are comforts that cannot be taken from me for six weeks at a time.

41

Outward-Bound Adventure

I don't know where those thirteen days went. They seemed to dry up and shrivel in the late spring heat wave until they completely evaporated. It was as if the fact that my sons and I wanted them to pass in slow motion had the opposite effect and made them go all the more quickly.

Before I knew it I was coping with suggestions from my ex about travel arrangements and packing. When he dropped off the airline tickets he asked, "Do the boys have luggage?" Wondering if he was going to offer to buy some because he couldn't know that I'd just splurged on a new set of American Tourister, I said, "Why do you ask?" He answered, "Well, if they don't, just fold their clothes in a box and ship it to us."

I nodded my head and resisted the urge to send all their belongings in Gucci or Vuitton to eliminate once and for all the constant "I'm so rich, you're so poor" reminders that ex-husbands mindlessly master so well. Instead, I began to sort clothes, placing them in my sons' bright red luggage and wonder how it is that, like cats, some men manage always, undeservedly, to land on their feet wearing an ever-present Cheshire grin.

The suitcases were packed with six weeks' worth of clothes, the travel documents and tickets and reservations were waiting on the nightstand, and we found ourselves, the night before departure, sitting on the bleachers watching my son play baseball. The announcement blared over the loudspeaker that my son, number thirteen, would leave the country the next day. Teammates and parents wished him well and we walked to the car with much hair tousling by the adults and fanny slapping by the kids.

The next morning, after hours of tossing and turning, the suitcases were in the car. I combed the boys' hair and checked and double-checked their clothes, an inordinate excessive number of times, and we reluctantly pulled out of the driveway en route to Los Angeles International Airport. Had anyone asked me, I would have imagined that our last few hours together would have been jammed with nonstop chatter and last-minute reminders; they were, instead, almost ominously quiet.

Worrying about our respective abilities to manage apart from each other—when we'd never been apart for more than a few days—we each had lists of instructions. I would ask the boys to call me collect whenever they got lonesome; one son would ask me to remember to buy a special brand of cat food for Tiger, the itinerant neighborhood feline, and the other would ask me to send him a box of his favorite homemade oatmeal cookies. And then again we'd be shrouded in silence and our own thoughts—as if we were using so much strength in being stoic that there was little left for conversation.

We arrived at the airport, parked, checked the baggage, and watched the planes as we waited for boarding time. I reminded the boys to take their vitamins every morning and brush their teeth three times a day. They reminded me to write them often and not to be afraid of "roughing it" while I lived all by myself. Pushed by a stampede of passengers we all too soon found ourselves on the plane and I reluctantly fastened seat belts around the plane's most precious cargo.

My five-year-old said, "Mommy, please stay on the plane with us so we can all go together." I hugged him and said, "I love you, baby, but I can't go with you." Then both boys, before I could disentangle myself from the seats and the pillows and the other passengers, began, simultaneously, to cry.

Countless hugs and kisses and I-love-you's later, I walk off the boarding ramp. I tell myself that the surprise games I've packed in their travel valise will occupy them on board and that the stewardesses will keep their cheerful promise to take good care of my sons. The scene had an eerie déjà vu about it, and I wondered how many Christmases and summer vacations would find me saying goodbye to my boys.

The walk to the parking lot takes forever, the drive home to Glendale takes forever, and the ability to stop sniffling and get the lump out of my throat takes even longer. I feel as if I've placed my whole existence on that jetliner and I console myself with the thought that anyone who had put their entire family on a foreign-bound plane for a six-week sojourn would be equally unnerved.

When I walked in the house I am met with almost deafening silence. There is no disorder, no noise, no footsteps. I lecture myself that summer visitation will be a six-week opportunity for me to catch up on my overdue writing assignments, to finish my book, to organize and streamline my life. I will, the lecture continues, approach it not as a month and a half chunk of time but day by day—as in "One Saturday Down—Five More to Go."

My friends and neighbors call to make sure I'm okay and regale me with cute stories of what the boys have told them about wanting to stay home instead of leaving the country. They urge me to be productive and to grow, and they make plans for dinners and movies and parties.

As I go about my chores I unpack the old pep talk to remind myself that sooner or later we each have to accept that we are ultimately alone in this life; I just happen to be forced to accept it sooner than most. I make my first visit to the boys' unoccupied room, so orderly it should be photographed for *House Beautiful,* and I hope against hope that they can feel my love for them—wherever they happen to be at this moment—as surely as I feel their little-boy love for me. I turn out their bedroom light, lock the doors, make a pot of coffee, and curl up on the couch. I tell myself that my sons and I, thousands of miles apart, are finally wading through our first weekend of this generation's Outward-Bound Adventure—an experience tailor-made to test today's broken-home families.

42

---◦◦◦◦◦---

Memoirs of a Childless Mother

Now that the boys are gone I can announce I'm on vacation. For the first time in my life, I am actually living alone. Always before I could count on coming home to a parent, a husband, or a child. Now I come home to no one. It has been a stark adjustment, from years of being both mother and father to not having a title at all. Here are a few things I discovered while I was left alone to lead an unfettered life:

I discovered that the nicest thing about having the boys gone was that I felt like a genuinely nice person—I never had to raise my voice, punish anyone, nag, correct table manners, or remind a child—for what seemed like the tenth time—that it was time to go to sleep, brush his teeth, make a bed, or do a chore. The vacation from being the in-house disciplinarian is so welcome.

I discovered that I never prepared a real meal while the kids were gone. Although we don't always have formal meals at our house, we rarely skip meals. This summer I learned how to snack, how to nibble, how to eat effortlessly. The stove and I practically became strangers. Only SOS requests from the boys to mail cookies sent me back to the oven in time to prevent me from completely forgetting how to function as a foodsmith.

I discovered that I could date without complications, I could disco, I could have men to the house, I could spend a night on the town, without worrying about the baby-sitter or tomorrow's early-morning baseball game. I could be femme fatale if I chose without feeling guilty over a little boy's missed good-night kiss.

I discovered that I'd unconsciously fallen into a pattern the past year of using my sons as shields. After they left there was no one to screen my phone calls, run errands, help with chores, lift my spirits, provide much-needed hugs and kisses, or say the words "I love you." I had to learn to fend for myself—physically and emotionally—in areas that I thought were of little concern. After feeding the cat for the hundreth time and wishing someone were around to enjoy the latest home-improvement job, I could no longer deny that my little men more than pull their weight when they're home and, contrary to popular opinion, make my life much easier in many ways—and that's some discovery.

I discovered that I suddenly had the spare time to redecorate the guest room, to give parties, to have house-guests, to take dance lessons again, and to enjoy long, hot bubble baths.

My schedule after a decade of motherhood catapulted me into a world I'd never known existed. My normal "rush" became "relax" and I learned that coordinating one life (instead of three) is far, far simpler than I'd ever, from my parental perch, believed possible.

I discovered that housekeeping sans enfants is a snap—nothing was scattered or dirtied or "lost" for six whole weeks! It was as if my home had been hermetically sealed when the children left. My usual routine of walking in from work and automatically rearranging and straightening and organizing as I made my way from one end of the house to the other was blessedly interrupted. For six weeks my hands did not touch a baseball, a hockey puck, a mitt, a basketball, a glove, a bat, a Frisbee, or a little boy's uniform. My home became a (too) quiet sanctuary for a single woman.

I also discovered a new and different type of loneliness, a brand that must be bottled especially for mothers. It is the loneliness of wanting to know, to observe, to share, to feel a part of your child's life—but being prevented from doing so.

The best discovery of all was finding that my sons and I could each return to our normal family life as soon as they stepped off the plane. Knowing that we missed each other and could still grow and be happy on our own was perhaps the most valuable lesson of the weeks I lived on my own for the first time.

43

---∙∙◦∞◦∙∙---

The Folly of Friendly Divorces

I had a phone call last night to inform me that a couple I've known for twelve years are filing for divorce. As if by reflex, I looked heavenward and gave thanks that I was here—on the other side of psychic survival—instead of in their shoes.

I have now been husbandless long enough to be over the hurt, the fear, and the shame I once felt so acutely. Now I find it hard to believe that I once was convinced that because I was a divorcée I was branded a failure at the marriage sweepstakes. Although every now and then I still feel a twinge of longing or regret, those feelings no longer occupy many of my waking thoughts. Not long ago they did.

Athough I was disappointed that my long-married friends were separated, I was even more sad to hear the wife say, "We've agreed to have a friendly divorce." Swell.

I'm happy that there wasn't a single "friendly" thing about my divorce—the words seem to me mutually exclusive, suitable for cataloguing next to "effortless exercise" and "painless torture." Not everyone agrees with me, of

course, but I believe now—as I did on the day I said "I do"—
that a marriage is not a union to be entered into lightly.
Everything in my background—parents, religion, relatives—
made it impossible for me to think otherwise. And if I
entered into wedlock as a matter of great import, how
could I be expected to pleasantly bid adieu to the man I
agreed to cling to unto death?

Which is why I've always been suspicious of those rare
(and the better you know the parties involved the rarer
they become) "cordial divorces." It's unnatural to turn a
strong, vibrant, powerful emotion inside out and find
something bland in its place. So I have reserved my feelings of sorrow not for the couples who rant and rave and
suffer seizures of *Angst*. Those who are calm and unfeeling
as they break apart present a much sadder scene because
they probably did not leave much emotion, commitment,
or desire behind.

I know that in those long-ago months when people discovered that I felt my husband was acting like a selfish,
lovesick jerk (and *he* felt I was vying for the shrew-of-the-
century award), our friends were shocked. After all, he
was the proper, ever-so-polite banker, and I was a typical
bookworm and would-be-writer. Two intelligent people
who had dated since sixteen and had literally grown up
together could surely subdue their feelings or hostility,
couldn't they? No.

So instead of a friendly divorce we had restraining orders, cancelled bank accounts, accusations and counter-
accusations. Now that it has all begun to dim into the
memory bank of past horrors, I feel that, painful as it was
at the time, it was the right way to sever our bond. If
nothing else, I know that once in my life I loved a man
with all my might and that he, until he felt the need to
look for love somewhere else, loved me too.

These are thoughts I rarely think because I'm a different woman now than I was when he left. Putting "good" or "bad" tags on the trauma of a buried marriage is not an activity I list among my current priorities. But the phone call from my friends has struck a lot of hidden emotion in me, and I wonder how I changed so many habits and perspectives and goals in so short a time. The only answer is: I was forced to restructure my every thought about love and life and the lessons they teach when I came face to face with losing what I had felt was a "sure thing."

So I say nothing to my dry-eyed friend who can survive the loss of a husband of many years without so much as a shriek or a sob. She tells me how reasonable and equitable and rational they will be as they divvy up the remnants of twenty years spent together. I still can't believe a single word she says. From where I stand, if love in its inception is not by definition "reasonable, equitable, or rational" how can it suddenly assume those qualities, like a deathbed conversion, at the moment of its demise?

44

---◦◦⟨∞⟩◦◦---

The Ageless Appeal of the "Older" Man

Although I've kept my romantic activities to a minimum since I became a single mother, I have had enough time to date, to flirt, and to fall in (and out) of love.

What I would like to share with you is a phenomenon I once thought was my own personal, secret preference. I'm learning, as I meet more and more single women, that I'm not alone in this peculiarity. The majority of men with whom I have spent time since my divorce bear several uncanny resemblances to each other. And they're becoming more and more similar to the men my girl friends are choosing to date. While I prefer to keep the nature of most of their similarities to myself, I can divulge that these men are, to begin with, almost always fifteen (or sometimes—gasp—more) years older than the women they date. Before you sputter and turn the page in disgust, please let me explain the circumstances of our attraction to the proverbial older man.

Not long ago I was reluctant to talk about this supposedly aberrant behavior, but the concept of safety in numbers has reinforced my initial hunch. I don't know exactly why an older man has that certain indefinable appeal—neither does Janie nor Sue nor Lynn—but I'm willing to take a few guesses.

The first advantage he has is the simple knack of knowing how to treat a woman like a lady. Some call it charm and others label it "politesse," but there's something to be said about a man who knows when to send flowers, how to select wines, or how to light a cigarette without making a fool of himself. When a man has lived long enough to get a few gray hairs he has also usually learned how to do a lot of the right things the right way. And most women—of any age—find that appealing.

The second advantage is the practical perspective of physical attraction. As in "you look awfully good to him." A thirty-year-old woman is going to look far better to a forty-five-year-old man than she will to a man her own age. Most thirty-year-old men are either married and learning how to cope with fatherhood or mentally undressing this year's entire crop of college graduates. When a woman begins to feel the bloom of youth fading a tad, a man of her own age who has yet to sport his first wrinkle won't help her feel younger than springtime. Sad, but true.

Another big plus, which could fill a book of its own, is that most older men are rarely intimidated or turned off by children. But the best thing about older men could simply be labeled "attitude." Anne Morrow Lindbergh once wrote that there are two types of men in this world— those who want to understand women and those who want to protect them. A lot of younger men are so busy establishing careers and exercising their new, improved executive egos that they're too busy with their own concerns to be interested in either understanding or protecting a woman.

A man who has been around a while is usually firmly established in his chosen career and has the time and interest to develop the side of his personality that's probably been neglected for the past ten to fifteen years—the fun side. This enables him to enjoy himself, to relax, and to be interested in what his woman has to say. An "older" man is not enthralled with the idea of using a date as his personal sounding board. While there will be no demands that a woman be svelte or sycophantic or even drop-dead sexy, he will almost always expect you to be interesting. And he is usually capable of being pretty interesting in return.

I call to mind encounters with men of my own age: One of whom asked me when I last weighed 100 pounds and was aghast when I honestly answered "eighth grade"; one of whom was literally incapable of speaking in complete (i.e., subject, verb, object) sentences and littered the evening with his "you know's" and "man's" and "really's" and "far out's"; one of whom expected me to pay for the movie since he'd paid for dinner and was shocked to learn I'd left my money—and my willingness to pay—at home; one of whom wanted me to drive and pick him up at his place because he didn't like to have to drive his prized expensive auto in nighttime traffic. No kidding!

While it's entirely possible that the aforementioned turn-offs could have occurred at the hands of older men, so far that hasn't happened. When I want a nice meal, interesting conversation, good manners, subtle wit, yes, and romance I have a hard time finding it in a man my age. Now that my divorced girl friends have begun to talk about such things, it seems that they do, too.

I had a dinner date last week with a very nice, very talkative "older" man who gave me further pause to won-

der about the appeal of someone from a different generation; I had trouble paying attention to much of what this
dear man was saying; he bore an uncanny resemblance to
someone from my past, but I couldn't remember who. By
the time we'd decided to splurge on L'Orangerie's apple
tart, I'd finally placed the face—my date looked like an older
version of good old Mr. Fillbrandt, a high-school English
teacher during my senior year who always gave me chal-
lenging assignments. Determined to see if my recollections
of Mr. Fillbrandt were correct, last night I unearthed my
dusty and long-forgotten annual.

I don't know about you, but my annual hasn't seen the
light of day during the seventies; as a matter of fact, it
hasn't been touched since my graduation from high school
back in the late 1960s. Opening the book gave me some
eerie sensations as well as a chance to look at an earlier me
with the benefit of 20-20 hindsight.

The book was full of the normal scribbles from class-
mates anxious to outdo each other by heaping inaccurate
compliments after my name. Much as I hate to admit it
(and contrary to what anyone who reads my annual might
believe), I was not "adorably sweet," "always cheerful,"
"wonderful," or "the nicest person in the class." Never
before—nor after—the annual signing day that long-ago
June were so many undeserved kudos heaped upon so
many by so many.

There were the usual messages from teachers, the compliments on my graduation-ceremony speech, the foreign-
language salutes from the polyglot teachers, and the urg-
ings from faculty members who were younger than I am
now to grow and study and change. And, just as I knew
he would be, there was a smiling Mr. Fillbrandt who
looked exactly the way I remembered.

There were the senior-class portraits—I can't believe

that I *ever* looked that young—of me and a lot of other people, all of whom thought that life and success and happiness were only waiting to be enjoyed, much like apples on a tree just waiting to be picked. The air of supreme confidence radiating from each photo makes me long to find out if Marie or Patsy or Sylvia hit—as I did—rough spots during the past decade or so.

Although I don't feel particularly older or wiser than when I wore the cap and gown and droned into the microphone that hot June night, I do feel more weathered. I feel that friends and lovers and children and co-workers have chipped and frozen and blasted until I've lost the sharp definitions and sense of unlimited possibility that once made people think I was such a star.

I know that for as long as I live I'll never again be able effortlessly to collect so many paragraphs of praise from my peers. Men today would die before they'd write in a book how much they "respect" me and women would probably rather scratch my eyes out before they'd glowingly describe their "envy." The days of shining it on and unabashedly saying things to make people feel good have drifted out of our lives, along with other teenage affectations.

Every now and then I miss the girl I used to be—who never looked over her shoulder or thought about protection from life's ups and downs. It was a short, short time ago when I felt that everyone loved me merely because I was alive, and the whole world was waiting only for me, for me, for me to show up so the party could begin.

I wish I'd thought to bottle a bit of the energy and optimism and self-confidence I had on graduation night. There are more than a few nights when a whiff or two might do me a world of good.

I reluctantly close the annual, return it to its dark and dusty cubbyhole, and wrestle with the mysteries of out-of-date dreams. If nothing else, it's certainly enough to make me wonder if one of the reasons I liked my "older" dinner partner as much as I did was because of his resemblance to a member of my long-ago, superstar, trouble-free life.

Whatever the reason, I can hardly wait to have dinner with him again.

45

———⋯⟨∞⟩⋯———

Opportunists

There are five women sitting in a small restaurant in Chinatown. It's the type of little restaurant that caters to women who work at office jobs in downtown L.A. The waiters are the only men these women can expect to be subservient and smiling and anxious to please. That's why it is such a popular place. In addition to good food and moderate prices it offers a one-hour role reversal for women who need a break from the stereotypes of the L.A. business world.

The women are talking about a breed of woman they know. This type of woman—you probably know one or two yourself—manages, with apparently little or no effort, to wrap men around her little finger. This type of woman is apparently born with a sixth sense—the ability to read men's minds. Since she knows how a man thinks, she can maneuver and manipulate him not only to give her what she wants but to also make him think it was his idea in the first place.

The women at the restaurant, none of whom have the slightest inclination to be *that* type of woman, are trying to categorize the qualities of their opportunistic sisters. Almost like a person watching an airplane, who doesn't want to be an airplane but is still fascinated by (and curious about) them. The women concur that a few essential opportunistic qualities are good looks, a nonthreatening demeanor, an ability to deceive oneself (and others), and a strong sense of "me first."

They chitchat about various friends or co-workers who seem to go through life taking from men until they get what they want and where they want to be. The women agree that Gloria Steinem was right when she spoke, long ago, of how women found it easier to achieve power through the men they "trapped" than to achieve it on their own through hard work and/or talent.

One woman, helping herself to another tea cake, reminds her luncheon companions that they're overlooking something—they're forgetting that men do—and have since time began—the same thing. But they do it in a much more subtle way.

"It is," she says, "as if they're professional opportunists. Women are still novices when it comes to any type of power at all, so we tend to be too blatant. But men—they've always known how to get what they want. I heard a story yesterday that illustrates my point.

"A young man from a middle-class neighborhood in Phoenix got married a few years ago. He was the star of his family and his neighborhood. He made fabulous grades, graduated with honors, was student-body president—the whole schmeer. On a liberal scholarship he trooped off to college and distinguished himself. He forsook the pleasures of fraternity life and limited his activities to a part-time job and pursuing the dean's list. By the time he graduated he was Phi Beta Kappa, summa cum laude, and the graduation speaker. He had sacrificed a full social life but he was quite a star in the eyes of the faculty. He was admitted to law school, again on a scholarship, and set about equaling his undergraduate performance. Meanwhile, back home, his parents bragged at every opportunity about their wonderful son Jonathan. Mr. and Mrs. Kapp had spent a lifetime training their son to get ahead in this world and it was finally beginning to pay off.

"Shortly before Jonathan graduated from law school he announced he was going to get married. He had met a young woman, Mildred Tailor Fownes (of *the* Fowneses) and it had been love at first sight. Millie would, after her junior year abroad, be returning to Vassar to finish her degree; after her graduation, she and Jonathan would marry.

"Jonathan began spending more and more time at the Fownes's estate in Virginia. Even though his parents didn't see much of their son (after all why should he return to Phoenix when he could enjoy the social advantages of the Fownes estate?), they were thrilled at the idea that their son was going to marry a socialite.

"After the wedding—so lavish that it was covered by *Town and Country* and *Vogue*—the Phoenix paper published a photo of "Ms. Mildred Tailor Fownes-Kapp" in heirloom veil and Givenchy gown. Jonathan effortlessly passed the bar, and the newlyweds settled into a small but very expensive home—a wedding gift from Judge and Mrs. Fownes."

To make a long story short, Jonathan joined the prestigious law firm where his father-in-law had once worked. But before he did, he quietly had his name (and his degrees and honors and awards) changed. There is no Jonathan Kapp listed in the membership of the Virginia Bar Association, no Jonathan Kapp in the phone directory—he has been replaced by Jonathan Fownes. He is now one of the Fowneses. He learned, perhaps back when his class-mates were screwing around at the Sigma Chi house, that some names have to earn power; other names get it free. Jonathan was tired of a lifetime of earning and figured it was time to let someone else do the heavy work. And finding the richest woman with the most influential father was the fastest way he could imagine to get to the top.

The kicker of the story is that his parents, in their two-bedroom house in Phoenix, still brag about how Jonathan, whom they rarely see, finally made it big in Virginia.

The women chipped in to pay the luncheon tab and walked back to the office through the laid-back bustle of the lunchtime crowd. The women exchanged disapproving adjectives about the man who sold his soul and his very name to get what he wanted—and the women who do the same day in and day out. They talked about the woman who no longer worked in their office who had pulled some pretty questionable stunts on her unsuspecting boyfriends and had done it with the utmost of ease and innocence.

The women were understandably depressed by the stories of these opportunists. They knew it would be next to impossible to put the war between the sexes on "hold" as long as there were men and women who made lifelong careers out of manipulating, for their opportunistic best interests, members of the opposite sex.

46

———— ⌒∞⌒ ————

Christmases

Although some things have remained constant throughout my life (such as my love for chocolate and horses and music), most affections have been fraught with change. Unfortunately, especially for someone so fettered by tradition, Christmas has not been a holiday marked with a sense of continuity. In fact, unlike our other holidays, it seems to change in at least one way every year.

The first Christmases I remember were right out of a storybook. My parents and I lived in a large white house on the edge of the forest in rural Oregon. At Christmastime my father and I would bundle up, trek through the woods until we found a tree I felt was perfect, and then daddy would chop it down. We'd drag the tree home through the snow, make sure it touched the living-room ceiling, and then reward ourselves with mama's eggnog and vanilla fruitcake.

When we left the forests of Oregon for the West's other small towns, we bought our touch-the-ceiling trees at neighborhood lots. The Christmas Eves of my youth would still be filled with midnight mass, daddy's at-home reading of the nativity scene from the Bible, permission to open one gift before bedtime, and then a serene Christmas morning with the three of us methodically opening gift after gift after gift.

When I married, my holidays were spent with my husband's large family, and I was introduced to a Christmas culture shock. The confusion of nine people in a small house created noise and bustle unlike anything I'd ever experienced. Last-minute wrapping and forgotten errands were in sharp contrast to the orderly, well-planned Christmases my family had known. The mountain of gifts created by nine or more people exchanging gifts, the little imitation tree, and the chance to talk, talk, talk with family became the order of the day for the next few years.

After my husband moved out, "the most joyous season" became something altogether different. Realizing my awkward status at *his* family's house, but having no family home of my own to retreat to, I relied on the generosity of friends who extended invitations to me for the Christmas Eves I didn't want to spend alone. One year, I entertained single out-of-town guests for the holiday; another I invited all my family-less friends to a communal Christmas feast prepared just the way my mother would have done. But every year there seem to be new quirks to change the way we celebrate the holidays.

Maybe the boys are away to visit their father or maybe they're here. Either out-of-town friends are houseguests or the three of us have the house all to ourselves. Either we spend Christmas Eve at the house of friends or we go to their traditional Christmas morning brunch. Either my son serves as altar boy at midnight mass or we go to church late the next day. The almost endless options grate on my nerves and make me long for a reliable traditional holiday that, just as in storybooks, remains the same year after year after year.

It was just such a longing that forced me to rearrange my expectations when I became a single mother. I'd never before been able to understand the statistics that warned of holiday suicides and Christmas depression. When my marriage broke up, I understood.

I had to learn that the holiday season brings up a mass of emotions and expectations, most of them unrealistic. The trap of sentimentality that surrounds us from Halloween to New Year's sets the stage for a case of seemingly terminal depression. Dreams of recapturing feelings and memories that shade recollections of bygone times led me on a merry—and hopeless—chase. The desire to have the "perfect" holiday (i.e., like the ones I used to have) nudged me into emotional, physical, and financial excesses. The holidays should help us feel better now—not feel better about something that is a dim reminder of an earlier life or an earlier love. I know, I know: easier said than done.

After my ex moved out, a twice-divorced friend gently chided me for my elaborate plans to have a Christmas for my children that would be a carbon copy of their earlier holidays. I reconstructed everything as perfectly as humanly possible. The only difference was that their father wouldn't be there; he would be with someone else.

As the boys and I were hanging up our personalized stockings, my then three-year-old son brought his father's stocking to me and tearfully suggested that we put it up anyway—otherwise Santa Claus wouldn't know where to leave daddy's treats. I learned, the hard way, that changing traditions—not *eliminating* them, just *altering* them—sidesteps many such painful scenes.

Now we have different wreaths, different ornaments, different stockings. We don't decorate the tree as a family of four—we decorate it as a large family of friends, many of whom are also alone. We celebrate joyously because these new traditions do not include any unnecessary reminders of the way we were. They represent a newfound satisfaction with the way we are.

It does help to be ruthlessly realistic—in spite of a natural sense of disenchantment. I had to remind myself that I would not be the only person to have a less than A-1 American holiday season. Taking the proverbial bull by the horns and including others in our celebration—single, married, or divorced—reaped genuine benefits. It was good for my children (and my friends) to learn that there is more than one way to celebrate Christmas. There doesn't have to be a daddy at the head of the table. Or a bustling, apron-clad mommy.

All we need now to enjoy the season of celebration is warmth and love, a sense of gratitude for what has been received in the past, and an air of optimistic expectancy about the future.

Every year my children compose extensive lists before we make our annual visit to Santa Claus. By the time the big event arrives, the list is memorized and recited in precise and excited bursts of enthusiasm. Each year the list becomes more elaborate, more specific, and more expensive. My boys indulge their wildest fantasies during the month of December and are genuinely awed to see—for one morning each year—many of those dreams come true.

This Christmas, I'm following their lead. I'm going to make a wish list, too. And I hope Santa listens to people over ten years of age!

I wish for all children, the gift of parents who listen.

Parents who are capable of taking the time to hear what a child says that's not put into words, who're anxious to find out what that little person needs (but won't ask for—whether it's time or love or discipline), who will try, no matter how hard, to be the best parent on the face of the earth. Just try.

I wish that every child could go to bed knowing that he or she is loved and respected and wanted; that kind of knowledge will transcend all the problems of money, grades, and growing pains.

I wish, for all parents, the gift of children who recognize that behind the seemingly glorious facade of adulthood are problems and never-ending headaches. Children who can accept that adults have disappointments and fears and annoyances that have nothing to do with children—but are shared with the child anyway, sometimes wisely, sometimes not.

I wish parents the joy of open communication with youngsters, and the ability to help a child understand that discipline and punishment and lectures exist not to make the adult feel powerful but because the only way to help a youngster grow, sometimes, is with a strong push toward obedience.

I wish for single people the gift of self-assurance, the gift of feeling worthy and beautiful and important, in spite of the fact that there isn't a "special someone" to give reassurance when you most need it—as at Christmastime.

I wish for happily married people the ability and wisdom to know how to help those families scarred by divorce. I wish for them the generosity of spirit to extend invitations, helping hands, and love to people who desperately need it but are usually too bewildered or proud to ask. I wish that families would remember that holidays are potentially depressing reminders of happier days, and that including a single person or a small family in your plans will do wonders for you both. And I wish that you always remain happily married.

For newlyweds and those who have found another mate (who may succeed where another didn't) I wish the.fortitude and the grace and the perseverance to find whatever it is that keeps couples (and families) together. I wish that you learn to respect each other for your good traits and try to work out the "bad" traits without affecting whatever magic it was that brought you together in the first place. May you celebrate Christmas giving thanks that you have each other, that you have an opportunity to make a go of a permanent relationship, and that you never forget that at one time you were alone and frightened and single. And that, unless you take each other very seriously, you may be that way again. I wish you a lovers' Christmas, full of romance and tenderness and magic—and I wish for it to be shared with everyone so we can all remember that Christmas is, after all, the season of love.

47

Lonely Nights

It is ten o'clock on another Friday night. It is raining. My younger son is safely tucked in the lower berth of his cow-boy-special bunk bed and a new stuffed puppy dog shares his sleeping space.

I am tucked in my Serta king-sized bed surrounded by frilly blue pillows, an abundance of reading matter, and an unsettling, unusually strong awareness that I'm alone.

The muffled giggles of my ten-year-old can be heard from the den. He has found—at last—a friend in the neigh-borhood whose father also left for other pastures. I can faintly hear them comparing notes on their life-styles, their mothers, their dreams, and their hurts.

Whenever I feel lonely I know it's Friday night. The rest of the week I'm too tired, too behind schedule, too programmed to admit—much less feel—loneliness. Along with banana splits and disorganized closets, loneliness is something I do not allow myself—unless it is Friday, unless it is raining, unless I have no romance in my life, and un-less everyone seems to have a someone except me.

I shift in bed—the chosen womb of my existence, where I

sleep, eat, read, write, and coordinate my not-so-together-life—and look at the side where "he" used to reside. It has now been many many moons since a husband shared that side of the bed, yet on rainy nights or during thunderstorms I instinctively feel that someone should be there. Someone to whom I can turn and explain why a paragraph made me laugh out loud. Someone who will notice that I'm wearing a new perfume, someone who will like the feel of my hair, or the wrinkles in my nose, or my nightly habit of writing in my journal.

After he left—to share someone else's bed—I noticed the bedroom becoming more and more feminine. Without a conscious effort on my part, lace appeared and down appeared and pastels and sachet and eyelet appeared. Now the man who slept beside me for a decade wouldn't recognize this room if he saw it. I have slowly, tangibly, acknowledged that it is no longer ours. It's mine.

In my little sanctuary I take grim comfort in the fact that I am one of thousands of lonely Friday-night women in the city. We're the people who cuddle next to pillows or children or dreams when the rain falls or the thunder claps or the wind whistles; we have full lives and happy times but there are plenty of times when we don't have a man on Friday nights.

John Leonard—a wordsmith of wondrous skill—once wrote an essay about New York women who, it turns out, are not all that different from their L.A. counterparts. Leonard wrote about the women who were bright and charming and unattached. He talked about these women and their departed husbands and then he talked about their aloneness. "The last thing they need is little boys, and the men in this city tend to be little boys, with wooden swords." But, since big men like younger and younger women, those of us who don't make a career of disco or a hobby of doting on daddykins are left to pursue other pleasures. Like big lonely beds on rainy Friday nights.

Leonard tells us of his women friends—who are wise and competent and complicated and lonely. "Everybody," he writes, "deserves better than this. It takes a long time and a lot of practice to become a human being. It is outrageous that, having finally done so, you discover that no other human being seems to need you."

I close the John Leonard book and turn off the lights. If I hurry to sleep I can wake up and it will be Saturday—which will mean that the next Friday is a good, safe, almost full week away.

48

Management vs. Labor and L.A.'s Single Women

I have dreamed, as have most writers, of having a special aerie where the problems of the world could be ignored and the muses welcomed. Anne Morrow Lindbergh has her outdoor shed and Adela Rogers St. Johns has her choice of a New York hotel room or a vista overlooking her beloved Pacific. I have borrowed typewriters, office lunch hours, and catch-as-catch-can spaces of free time to jot down notes. Sometimes on the minibus I sit scribbling, sometimes I jot down notes and ideas as I stand in line at the bank, and sometimes—usually—I write sprawled in bed next to coffee and cookies and the accompanying noise of two energetic boys.

If I could escape the tumult of the workaday world, my thoughts might be more serene and more ethereal. As it is, I'm right down there with the troops; too often what I want and need to say isn't fit to print. Today I'd like to share the most upsetting incident of my week. Getting it off my chest won't change the situation, but it'll absolve me from incurring Dante's wrath by virtue of having done at least *something* in a time of crisis.

Although I know that more and more working women
are assuming jobs of great import, such is not the lot of my
friends. With the exception of a female executive here and
a lady lawyer there, most of my college-educated, bright,
and charming friends work in dead-end office jobs. These
jobs make up the working lives of the faceless masses of
secretaries and receptionists and helpmates of the business
world, who work without fanfare, without large salaries,
and without perks that seem to flow like manna from
heaven to the women executives we read about. Take it
from me, those women are few and far between. Most
women—college educated or no—will spend a part (if not
most) of their working time trapped between a typewriter
and a telephone. It pays the bills, it buys the cars, and the
clothes, and the vacations, but it is not—by any perverse
stretch of the imagination—glamorous. Work, particularly
for women in offices, is just that: *work.*

Okay. Now that I've set the scene, let me tell you why
I'm upset. One of the loveliest young women I know, I'll
call her Eleanor, has worked for a large L.A. insurance
firm for five years. She is the person in charge of cataloguing accidents for the public-safety department. It is her
job to be friendly to people who call to find out why the
premium was so high, to be patient with executives whose
egos are ruffled by unflattering letters to them from irate
customers, and somehow to manage to treat the media with
kid gloves and a perfect smile.

These are not simple chores, but if anyone were ever
made for such a job it's Eleanor. The rest of the women at
her company have marveled for years at her inbred ability
to smile, to listen, and to cope with the pressures of her so-
called statistical job. The one thing Eleanor—and the many
women like her—cannot cope with is intraoffice treachery.

Eleanor would have stayed in her department for the

rest of her working life—the people in the company were nice, she was popular and enjoyed the camaraderie of her co-workers, and the pay was, if not gargantuan, enough to pay for her apartment rent, her used and slightly dented Toyota, and her annual vacation. At thirty-five, Eleanor had learned the hard way not to ask for too much in this life.

The sticky wicket of this story arrives in a person I'll call Brad. Brad is a young Ivy League would-be executive hungry for power. He was hired last year to "streamline" the department where Eleanor works. His first official act, after six months on the job, was to eliminate the top female in the department—a woman who had worked for Aetna, Prudential, and Fireman's Fund, and could tabulate data in her sleep. She was well-groomed, articulate, a top-notch statistician and responsible for a good-sized chunk of the department's output. She was, alas, also old enough to be Ralph's mother. So she was his victim number one.

Six months later, Eleanor is notified that because she can't take shorthand she is going to be replaced—she is ordered to find a position in the firm to which she might transfer or else face termination. The fact that no one in her position for the past ten years has ever had—or needed—shorthand is unimportant. The fact that Eleanor is a hard worker who gives the company a better image than all the Gregg scribbles in the world is also unimportant. The fact that a young man straight out of school who wants to establish his own empire has been brought into the department is important. Eleanor is victim number two.

When I hear stories like this I become ill. When I sit and watch them I become furious. I rankle at the enforced subjugation of women to would-be tyrants like Brad. I do a slow burn at the fact that without an independent

source of income or security, women with good work records and sweet dispositions can be squeezed, coerced, and
pushed out of jobs they want and deserve. Men like Brad
know how to protect themselves from lawsuits and gossip
and retribution—or at least they like to think they do.

The most frustrating part of the question is that I don't
know how to make any of this come to an end. How do
women see to it that snots from Ivy League schools with a
longing for power learn to respect skills of more than one
kind? How do women get shackled to jobs—like typing or
adding columns of figures—that prevent men in offices
from seeing them as anything other than automatons? How
do the personal empires of little men manage to overpower
kindness and generosity of spirit and satisfaction in a job
well done?

I don't know any of the answers. Neither does Eleanor
nor the other single women in cities whose grasp on a paycheck is far more tenuous than they might care to admit.

49

---·◦∞◦·---

One in Ten Is the Best
You Can Hope For

On a Friday night not long ago, I learned a valuable lesson. I'd had a bad week—no, to be honest, I'd had a bad month. Two magazines had simultaneously turned down articles (something so calamitous had never before happened) ; an editor whom I worshiped betrayed me; a friend I hoped would spend time with me was "too busy"; the boys were away on one of their weekends with their father; and a man who was the object of a full-blown, rather teenage crush, had chosen to see me as a friend instead of lover. Things were very bad indeed.

Because I had no idea that my ego would suffer so many rebuffs in one four-week period, I had earlier, with great confidence, planned a party for that doomsday Friday night. By the time my guests arrived I wanted to place my head—instead of the entrée—in the oven. Although others could see me as a successful, happy woman surrounded by friends, good food, and ample wine, I, of course, saw myself as an abject failure. My writer's ego had been crushed, my income had been halved, my self-confidence and optimism demolished. Pasting a Pollyanna smile on my face,

I somehow stumbled through the night pouring wine, greeting people, smiling, nodding, and wanting to slip between the floorboards.

Fear of failure and the specter of financial disaster reared up. I succumbed to their threats. My future seemed to consist (in my all-too-vivid imagination) of a calendar whose pages are rapidly flipped, as in old-time movies. Each page said "bleak—bleaker—bleakest" until, on the last day of the year, heavy black letters spelled THE END.

Walking from one room to another I could imagine the same people (in the future) nodding their heads as they left what had been my funeral mass at good old Holy Redeemer. Dear, trustworthy Monsignor Collins would have delivered a tear-jerking eulogy, my sons' schoolmates would have sung with choirboy sweetness. People would murmur to each other "she might have been a successful writer, if only (1) editors had been trustworthy, (2) magazines had printed her articles, or (3) she had had more talent."

I was roused out of this maudlin reverie by a guest who wanted more wine. I refilled his glass and then, his businessman's reserve loosened by the evening's alcohol consumption, he asked why I looked so sad. Had I not known—or liked—him so well, I might have tried to lie my way out of being caught feeling sorry for myself. Instead, I told him the month's list of ten or twelve mini-catastrophes that had caused me to sink lower and lower until I'd arrived at my present state of depression.

He listened, sipping his wine, and when he could finally get a word in edgewise, he gave me a lecture I won't soon forget.

"You know," he said, "I make a lot of money each year." Knowing his beautiful home and fully aware of how much I enjoyed shopping with his gorgeous wife, I couldn't help but admit that he was correct. "I sell computers, big jobs that cost a fortune and carry a damn good commission. And I could write a book about the heartaches I face. You word people aren't the only ones who suffer, you know. Just like you, I've got a family to support—they like trips to Europe, private schools, pretty clothes, and a nice car. And I'm more than happy to give them that and more. But nobody comes to me and gives me the dough to buy those things year after year. I have to do what you have to do—I have to sell."

I started to explain that I wasn't a saleswoman, I was a writer, but before I could say a word he cut me off. "Listen, kid, just remember that when you sell you're never going to be successful with everyone. The very best odds I'll give you, or me, or anyone, is one in ten. It's the best you can hope for. For every sale I make, I automatically figure that I'll get nine noes. So if I need to make ten sales a month to get by, I plan to give it my best a hundred times. And a long, long time ago I learned a lesson you obviously don't know. I learned to let the noes roll off my back. I learned that every 'no' brings me that much closer to an eventual 'yes,' and I never, ever take it as a personal rejection. It's just the odds, kid, one to ten is what you got to shoot for."

He asked for more wine, looked out at the moonlight on the garden, and before he left the room he said, "I know you're sad; hell, when I was your age I used to fall to pieces too. Just remember that for every ten mud balls you throw on a wall one of them will stick. And if you stay at it, you'll eventually cover the wall. Most people, the people who don't make it, walk away or run out of mud or spend more time cursing the mud than slinging it. I've read your stuff and I'm not losing any sleep over your ability to feed the kids or make your dream come true. But I'm going to ask you to promise me that no matter how many noes the bastards give you, you'll never stop throwing the mud. Promise me that, and I'll go back and let you finish dinner."

Somewhat taken aback, I promised, I served dinner, and I mulled over his words for quite some time. And as much as I dislike comparing the work people love—dentistry, medicine, law, dance, music, writing, art, or whatever— to "mud," I think my slightly inebriated friend's analogy is among the most helpful advice I've ever received.

Since that party, I've received a few "yeses" and a few "noes." But for some reason, I haven't been moved to slit my wrists when someone doesn't act the way I want them to act. These days, when people slam doors in my face I just grit my teeth and get ready to start slinging mud and more mud and more mud until, eventually, I hit my one in ten. After all, that's the very best odds I could get.

50

———⟨∞⟩———

Tim and Rona

I had lunch with my friend Tim last week. He'd asked me to meet him because he said he was feeling low and needed a friendly sounding board. Tim has been divorced for three years, has two sons, and is still in the process of making postbreakup discoveries.

When I asked him exactly why he was so blue, he unloaded the story of his most recent escapade in singlehood. "I'm depressed," he began, "because I just discovered that I'm as vulnerable as the next person to romantic daydreams that lead nowhere. And I'm getting pretty discouraged about the dormant state of my love life." I was surprised to hear this because I've assumed that men have little trouble in that department—they do the asking and women do the waiting. Tim was determined to destroy my ill-founded stereotypical beliefs.

"I've had my share of one-night stands and short-term affairs. Now I'm really hungry for the kind of intimacy I had with my wife. I want to have someone with whom I can share jokes, someone to go Saturday shopping with, someone who'll still be around next month or the month after that. But it's not so easy.

"You know, when I was in college, it was a cinch to have a girl friend. Now it's next to impossible. Either the women turn me off, or we live too far apart to make dating practical, or they don't like me. I'm beginning to wonder if I'll ever find someone with whom I can mesh." I nodded to let Tim know that I knew exactly what he meant.

"The worst thing that happened was when I called a friend of a friend. My friend works with this woman, Rona. He dared me to call her. You see, she's just coming out of a divorce and he thought I might like to take her to a show. So, since it was a dare, I did. We talked and found that we had a great deal in common. She was busy that weekend but I called her the next week and we had another great conversation. I liked her over the phone—or if I didn't like her, I at least liked the idea of laughing about the dumb things kids do, and we'd both gone to SC so we knew some of the same people and could laugh about old campus stories.

"I got to feeling real cozy on the phone just sharing—I hadn't been able to do that with many women since Sandi moved out. It was fun talking to Rona about the different restaurants and movies we'd each gone to, and before I knew it, I was really eager to take this woman out. I was beginning to be happy as hell that I'd made that bet. So the next time I called Rona, I suggested we go out to dinner the following Saturday night. She said she'd try to get a baby-sitter and asked me to call her the next night to firm up the time. I hung up feeling handsome and optimistic and happy to be alive. I felt that maybe I wasn't a freak—maybe someone could fall in love with me after all. It sounds stupid now, but I swear that's how I felt.

"I was feeling so good that I called my old fraternity brother Barry. He'd known Rona in college and I thought he'd get a kick out of learning about my new telephone relationship with her. What a mistake! Barry couldn't believe I'd asked her out. 'Don't you know,' he said, 'that she is so heavy into coke she can't see straight? Don't you know she's still into that primal scream and est and Rolfing stuff? That lady is trouble city, Tim.' I couldn't believe it, so I called the guy who had given me her number in the first place. I asked him if what Barry had said was true. He said he thought it was, so I asked why he even bothered to set me up with someone who was so kooky and unorthodox in the first place. He told me he was under the impression that I was looking for a fun night—not a partner for life."

Tim stopped talking. I broke the silence and asked, "Did you call back to discuss the dinner date for Saturday night?"

"You know," Tim said, "part of me didn't want to date someone my friends felt was weird, part of me wanted to date her in spite of what they felt, but another part of me just wanted to maybe go on believing that there really isn't someone out there to mesh with. It's a lot easier to get by if you don't keep hoping to find someone. So I just never called her back."

I felt sad after hearing Tim's story—sad for men who're tired of playing make-believe bachelor and sad for people who put so much stock into hearsay. But most of my sadness was reserved for Rona. With her baby-sitting arrangements made and her dinner date in the works, she'll never understand why the nice man named Tim didn't call her back.

51

---∙∙∞∙∙---

Discovering I'm Really Better Off Without Him

Sooner or later it happens to every divorcée. The moment it dawns on you, you can expect to experience a feeling akin to a personal apocalypse. The sky will part, the sun will shine, birds will sing, and music will fill the air. Your life will never be the same again.

I am speaking of the moment when you first realize that you really are better off without the husband you lost. During the painful period of mourning or the bitter siege of anger it's natural to fight against the reality that you—as a person of dignity and worth—do not need the presence of a partner who sees you as his personal ball and chain. It takes a long—too long—time to be able to bid "good riddance" and turn your smiling eyes elsewhere but, believe me, that time finally does come.

My personal moment of truth was not as earth-shaking an event as it could have been. During our drawn-out drama of separation versus divorce, even his least gentlemanly behavior rolled off my back without a moan of protest; it seemed as if there wasn't anything he could do to assuage my longings to have him back home. I was so

anxious to save my marriage and keep a daddy in the house
that he probably could have got away with murder before
I would have realized that being on my own was not, as I
had been led to expect, the worst of all possible fates.

As T. S. Eliot could have told me, the end of my admira-
tion and longing for my ex would come "not with a bang
but with a whimper." The straw that finally broke my al-
legiance is a short tale so full of irony that my friends have
insisted I write about it.

To begin: It is essential to the story to know that my ex is
a man of great entrepreneurial talent. I like to think that
my family's real estate connections and the fact that I
worked so that he could go to graduate school aided somewhat his accumulation of what is, by now, a very handsome
portfolio of properties. In the fifteen years I've known this
man, his net worth has gone from here to there. All very
impressive. While he grew up in small rented homes, he is
now landlord to many. The clothes he wears these days are
custom-made and monogrammed and his car is the latest
model. As a vice president for a large bank, one might say
that he is the embodiment of the Horatio Alger ethic.

He lives with his new wife in another country, thousands of miles away. His visits are brief, are becoming
less and less frequent, and are often bank-paid business
trips. His home is large, equipped with household help,
and his salary is handsome. The club enjoys his membership, and his new wife's family and their construction company will be able to help his land-development business far
more than mine did.

Almost three months after one of his trips to L.A. the
phone rang early one morning. In between making hot
chocolate and stirring Malt-O-Meal I lifted the receiver and
heard the ever unwelcome crackle of foreign long-distance
static. It was my ex telling me when he planned next to be

in town, what he would do with the boys, and what time he wanted them to be ready. When all the logistics were settled, I told him I had to get off the phone and head for the office.

"Wait," he said, "don't hang up! I have something important to ask you."

The sense of urgency in his voice led me to imagine fatherly concerns about the state of the boys' health, news of a surprise he'd planned for them, or perhaps he'd been wondering if the child-support checks were large enough to care for their needs. No such luck.

"Do you remember the last time I brought the boys home?" he asked.

"Let's see," I said racking my memory, "you mean three months ago?"

"Yes. Well, that day, B's socks were wet so I let him borrow a pair of mine to wear . . . ," he began.

"Oh," I said, "I didn't know."

"Yes. Well, since I'm coming to town I want to pick them up. They're brown. Would you wash them and pack them with the boys' clothes? I'll get them when I pick up the boys."

I explained to the poor man that I didn't know that he'd let my son borrow a pair of socks but that I'd be sure to get to the root of the problem. Barely suppressing a giggle I said good-bye and handed the phone to my hosiery-harboring son so he could speak with his father. The moment I got off the phone I knew that my emotional umbilical cord had been cut—forever.

It's hard for me to decide if the problem is with the devaluation of the dollar, or if the new club dues have hit harder than expected, or if the cost of men's socks (and interfamilial loans) has skyrocketed. I'm going to check into it, though, because whatever could cause a well-to-do businessman to worry about a single pair of socks—for any reason—for three months has got to be big stuff indeed!

I learned some important lessons from that phone call: I might have learned that men with money get that way through design rather than happenstance; that Laertes's advice still applies to certain twentieth-century fathers; or that wardrobe worries affect men as seriously as their most fashion-conscious female counterparts.

But the best lesson of all was that traits I once saw as admirable—like devotion to the dollar sign—were viewed that way by me only because I lacked objectivity about someone I loved. Once I saw the trait apart from the title "husband," it was clear that penny-pinching was something I could easily do without.

I owe a lot to that pair of socks, wherever they are, for they abolished forever my forlorn feelings of "what if."

My son has searched and searched for the brown socks. No luck. If he ever finds them I'd like to frame them and hang them on the wall. I must admit that ever since that early-morning phone call, I've been feeling like nothing less than the luckiest lady in L.A.

52

---·⊶∞⊷·---

Hopelessly Out of Step
with the Times

The closer we get to the twenty-first century, the more obvious it becomes that my life has been an ongoing testament to the past. More and more, I find that wherever "my head is at" just happens to be a few years behind—or ahead—of others; I never seem to be in synch with the times.

I was deeply into de Beauvoir before Gloria Steinem was a household word. I was entrenched in the joys of motherhood when my friends were praying that electric typewriters and Xerox machines would somehow make them sterile, and though I jogged each night, alone, back in '74, my friends now endlessly urge me to join them. The only exercise I indulge in these days is pushing typewriter keys and turning pages. No wonder I worry about being out of step!

These days, when I talk of how I feel about the state of womanhood, I'm met with blank, incredulous stares. Either no one has heard the things I say before, or else there is no desire to hear them now. How can this be, I wonder? Didn't their mothers ever talk to them—really talk? The impossibility of finding the teeniest bit of reinforcement for my beliefs has led me on a merry chase that resembles messianic zeal. I'm beginning to understand how cults begin.

My feelings about women were shaped, naturally, by watching my mother. Born near the turn of the century, she was in her late forties when she and my father adopted me. She had lived the life of a gay young thing in the twenties. I can clearly remember her smile as she told me of her numerous pairs of satin dancing shoes of different colors (for what must have been that era's equivalent of today's discos). She married my father in the less than lucky year of 1929.

It was the end, for both of them, of unlimited money, expensive new cars, trips, and extravagant wardrobes. It was a time to test their inner resources. I felt that my father, whose family lost a small fortune, never really recovered. Although he always seemed witty and entertaining during his last two decades, I could easily sense that the man I saw was only a shadow of the suave and daring pre-Depression fellow my mother had married.

She had lost as much money as he in the crash, but it didn't break mama's spirit. It curtailed her dreams, but it also gave her an opportunity to prove one of her pet theories: Women might appear to be soft, but inside they were of the finest mettle—they had to be, because people were always depending on them in ever so many small ways. By the time World War II began, my reticent, painfully shy mother had quietly proved her strength and her inner confidence to all.

Growing up with parents who were literally old enough to be my grandparents gave me experiences that are lightyears from what I see between parents—particularly mothers—and children today. I sometimes wonder if it was the mere accumulation of years that made my mother so different from my peers' moms, or if it was the way she had been raised by her parents.

The basic quality I have trouble finding among women today is a sense of dignity and a semblance of true strength. I see lots of bravado, lots of talk, even lots of anger—but I don't see an inner core of unbending pride in these women. Maybe that concept is too out of date to appeal to a generation that's at home with phrases like "sex-role stereotyping," "male chauvinism," and "capitalist oppression."

I look to my past and remember my mother firmly believed that men—because they were called upon to be charming and bright and capricious—were full of vulnerabilities that had to be protected. The very traits that allowed them to affect goodwill and gentlemanliness sprang from the strength of women—their mothers, their wives, their secretaries. For this reason, my mother (and, quite possibly, most of the women of her generation) knew better than to assume that they could stroll through life without plans or goals or restrictions. They knew there was no "wife" in the wings on whom *they* could really depend if need be. "Behind every great man is a good woman" was more than a slogan to my mother and her peers—it was a source of pride and a testimony to their power.

My women friends judge themselves on paychecks, titles, and job responsibilities—and I don't see all the difference, in spite of the brouhaha they raise—between getting one's ego massaged and reinforced by a "corporate man" than by a "family man." I'm probably just too hopelessly behind the times to understand.

Earlier generations of women didn't perceive power as the right to work as longshoremen; nor did they ask to find recognition in careers outside the home. Power for them centered around people—their people. They felt that it was crazy to earn a paycheck at the risk of missing the chance to shape a child's mind. The moral, intellectual, and spiritual character of the family was *their* "corporate" world. I think they took the job every bit as seriously as today's career women do theirs.

When I talk to my friends about my mother's strong opinions, about the things that were and were not a waste of time (beauty shops, Junior League luncheons, and credit cards were—cleanliness, nutritious foods, and books were not), they laugh at her simplemindedness. Women like her—are there any left?—regarded the well-being of their children and husbands as their career. It was a sacred duty, in those days, to have children; the health, education, and moral fiber of young ones was viewed as a covenant—not as a drag, a bore, a curtailment of one's personal freedom. The difference between these women's homes and husbands and offspring and those of today was their mode of expression. From where I stand, it seems to have been relatively individualistic. The unique quality they shared in their families centered on one word: pride.

The task of shaping people's lives was given to women, my mother believed, because men weren't quite strong enough for such a time- and energy-consuming job. I think she saw men as flashy four-hundred-yard sprinters, full of dash and razzle-dazzle. Women, on the other hand, were like the marathoners—steady and consistent and able quietly to outdistance the best. The trouble with that kind of woman, of course, is that if you didn't stick around for a long time you'd miss the beauty of their performance because it was overshadowed by the showiness of the men they loved.

I am supremely grateful that I had the opportunity to be raised by a woman who was among the last of a dying breed. Even among the few women I see today who are satisfied with Kinder, Kirche, Küche, there is an air of temporary commitment—it's only "until the children are raised." The banner of the ERA and the alleged thrills of the workaday world have reached them and started small stirrings of self-doubt. They're among the minority and they know it. I fear that the zeal my mother attached to my father, to me, our home, our meals, and her rose garden may never be seen again.

People no longer believe that "the hand that rocks the cradle rules the world." The deportment and health and well-being of children—or themselves—is no longer a source of pride (or shame) for far too many women. If a child does poorly in school or treats adults disrespectfully or shows no concern for other people's property, today's woman can shrug her shoulders and blame Freddy Silverman and poor TV programming. Feelings of approval or accomplishment can be won outside the home—so why bother with the ever-so-difficult job of housebound challenges? Is it any wonder that children see little reason to respect women—mothers—when they view with how little respect their own mothers regard their basic maternal responsibility?

Like the proverbial voice crying in the wilderness, I fear I may once again be alone. Other women of my age, perhaps because their mothers were twenty years younger than mine, may not have had a childhood with an honest-to-God career mother. Others may feel, as I once did, that their good-hearted mothers wasted their lives and foreclosed their options for a full life. I do not know.

It just seems that somehow—even though inflation, divorce, and today's androgynous life-style make it difficult—we should be able to celebrate a woman's pride and strength, and the dignity of nurturing a family to the best of one's ability. I guess I was raised to believe that "women are this country's finest asset" far too long to be able to think otherwise—even if it makes me out of step with the times. As usual.